Passage From India:

Post-1965 Indian Immigrants And Their Children

— Conflicts, Concerns, and Solutions —

Priya Agarwal

Yuvati Publications
P.O. Box 3251
Palos Verdes, CA 90274

Acknowledgements

My sincere gratitude goes to everyone who participated in this project—either by being part of the sample, by critiquing several drafts of the written version, or simply by providing moral support. Special thanks to the following people:

The individuals who were part of the sample for being generous with their time and open to sharing their concerns. This book is a product of their efforts.

Professor David B. Abernethy of Stanford University for his guidance, enthusiasm, and support, without which this project would not have been possible.

Laura Selznick and Stanford University Undergraduate Research Opportunities for a substantial grant that enabled me to pursue the project at this scale.

Subodh Chandra for being instrumental in taking a vague idea that originated in the Coffee House and making it real.

Sally Cole and Kathy Wright for their invaluable advice and friendship.

Terry Andrews, Gary Stapley, and Wayne Marshall for being indispensable in the production of this book.

Ankur J. Goel for allowing me to pick his brain on anything and everything even remotely related to second generation Indians.

Andrew P. Sieler for being the "salt of the earth" and the most insightful person I know.

Dina T. Figueroa for being my Stanford "soulmate" who put up with me through all of this.

Keshini T. Kashyap for being my favorite *un*confused *desi* and for helping me keep the faith.

Robin J. Koss, Carrie M. LaLonde, and Michelle D. Miguelez for making me believe I could do this and for proving Emerson correct when he said, "A friend may well be reckoned the masterpiece of nature." bff

Puneet R. Agarwal, my brother, for his humor, intelligence, and love—"Don't forget that your family is gold."

For my mother and father

Preeta and Vijay K. Agarwal

TABLE OF CONTENTS

Chapter IV
FINDING A PLACE IN AMERICA

Chapter V
PARTICIPATION IN AMERICAN SOCIETY

Chapter VI
CONCLUSION

PREFACE

OBJECTIVE

The purpose of this book is two-fold: to chronicle the history of professional Asian Indians who immigrated to the United States after 1965, as well as to point out the differences between these immigrants and their children (most of whom were raised in the United States) in social, economic, and political attitudes. Studying the second generation, the children of immigrants, reveals much of what the future could hold for this community. A description of the feelings and concerns of both generations, moreover, may help each group become more sensitive toward the other.

SIGNIFICANCE

Why study this community at all? After all, professional Indians still constitute a relatively small population in the United States and have been a presence in this nation for only 25 years. Yet Indians in the U.S. demand our attention at this juncture for several reasons. First, as an immigrant community they are distinctly different from both the earlier wave of European immigrants to the United States as well as from more recent immigrant groups. On the aggregate, Indians who immigrated in the wake of the 1965 Immigration Act were highly educated and technically-skilled professionals who, in a relatively short period of time, found themselves in the middle and upper socio-economic levels in American society. They were not refugees and did not establish "ghettos." They were, in fact, welcomed in the United States because of their professional skills or potential technical contributions. Yet their social, civic, and political involvement in mainstream American society is not commensurate with their professional success. Most intend to remain in the United States permanently; yet, in many ways, they have not broken their ties with India. Indians are distinct from other minority groups in that physically they have what some would call a "non-white, non-black" appearance. Furthermore, although India forms a major part of the sub-continent of Asia, Indians are not popularly considered Asians—that term being reserved primarily for East Asians.

The second significant aspect of this project is that it addresses an increasingly important segment of the American mosaic on which little academic work has been done. Ronald Takaki's recent book *Strangers From a Different Shore*, for instance, was considered a "panoramic overview of Asian American history." Yet, hardly four pages were devoted to the professional Indian immigrants whose numbers may be close to one million in the 1990 Census. This study, therefore, aims to document the thoughts and perspectives of this immigrant group while such an endeavor is still possible. In the following chapters, some of the questions that many Indians are asking *themselves* about the evolution and future of their community in the United States will be addressed. This study may act to redirect the community. As one interviewee stated, "We sit quietly and try to deal with our problems by ourselves. Yet, by looking at the big picture [of Indians throughout the United States], we will probably see that many Indian immigrants and their families share the same concerns. If we can see this, we will come out on top."

Third, the project reveals something about *American* society. In a sense, this is a study in political culture. Which facets of American society do immigrants and their children feel most comfortable making their own? Which aspects do they shun? The answers shed light on contemporary assimilation theory.

OTHER INDIAN IMMIGRANTS

It is important to distinguish between the professional Indian immigrants isolated for this study and other people of Indian origin in the United States. The early 1900s, for instance, saw a wave of immigrants from the Indian state of Punjab, hired as farm laborers in parts of California, Washington, and Canada. For several decades, these laborers faced intense and widespread discrimination. A majority of these men married Hispanic women, as laws prohibited their choice of marriage partners[1]. The descendants of these early immigrants, as well as others who later migrated as farm laborers, still constitute a substantial population in parts of northern and central California. Because they have been here for several generations, their concerns are different than those addressed in this study.

Similarly, since the relaxation of immigration laws in 1965, more non-professionally educated Indians have been coming to this country. Many are relatives of professionals and others already established here. These immigrants comprise much of the merchant class, operating motels, restaurants, grocery stores, liquor stores, and other "mom and pop" establishments. As they are more recent immigrants and because they lack professional backgrounds, their concerns are also very different from the group discussed in this study.

A GENERATIONAL STUDY

Although there are many labels that can be used to describe immigrants and their children, for the purposes of this study the term "first generation" will be used to describe the immigrants, and "second generation" will refer to their children.

The primary focus of this project is the generational and cultural chasm evident between immigrants and their offspring. In the initial stages of the study, it seemed that many more

[1] *Takaki, p. 310*

issues relevant to the professional Indian community, such as discrimination, civil rights, and a variety of political concerns, should be included. Yet, as more interviews were conducted, it became clear that at this point in the community's evolution—a juncture at which the second generation is just entering adulthood—the immigrants' main concerns are their children, specifically the children's ability (or inability) to balance two cultures that often preach seemingly diametrically opposed approaches to life.

The second generation, furthermore, despite its success in academics and other tangible measures of adolescent achievement, is concerned about its own psychological well-being. They often refer to themselves as "guinea pigs." Lacking role models within their own ethnic group, they are an experimental generation expected to chart their own course of adaptation and assimilation. Whom will they marry? How will they reconcile their bi-cultural backgrounds? To what degree will they pass their Indian culture on to the third generation? These are questions both generations are directly confronting as they straddle two distinct cultures. Perhaps by understanding the plethora of uncertainties and dilemmas faced by this younger generation, an effort can be made to assist young Indian-Americans in the process of forging their identities. Similarly, a greater degree of sensitivity can be generated toward the concerns of the immigrants.

Chapter III focuses on the second generation and is the focal point of this study. This section describes critical issues such as cultural and attitudinal differences between the first and second generation. This portion of the study also provides some suggestions to help immigrants and their children through this sometimes difficult period.

Project Design

Few in-depth sources are available on this topic. Since there is little documented information and analysis on the Indian-American community, most of the information for the study was obtained from primary sources, specifically through personal interviews with a sample of people from the community. Detailed information on the nature of and selection of the sample is included in Appendix A.

Two samples were taken for which there were two distinct questionnaires: one for first generation immigrants, another for second generation children (see Appendix B). One hundred and twenty individuals from each generation comprise the sample from which the statistics in this study are derived. The names of all individuals interviewed are changed within the text, with the exception of the names of community leaders. Unless indicated otherwise, all quotations within the text are from personal interviews. The fictitious Mehta family described in Chapter I is a portrayal of the concerns of Indian immigrant families in the United States. Quotations in this section are not taken directly from interview data but paraphrase the sentiments expressed in these interviews.

"TELL THE STORY"

My decision to pursue this project is the result of a desire to "tell the story" of Indian immigrant families in this country so that the beliefs, emotions, talents, and experiences of this group are not forgotten. This work is an effort to preserve their history as sensitively and authentically as possible.

It is important, nevertheless, to address the problems implicit in studying a community of which I am a part. To render this project more effective, I was naturally committed to remaining objective. This goal became difficult and trying at times. In some instances, the difference between how things *are* and how things *should be* became somewhat blurred for me. I feel, however, that I have been successful in my efforts to remain objective. My status as a second generation Indian may have affected the way in which interviewees reacted to me. In the most positive sense, I feel that being of Indian background enabled me to isolate issues of importance, as many of these issues stem from the experiences of the Indian-Americans who have been an important part of my life.

Not that the story need be long, but it will take a long while to make it short.

— Henry David Thoreau

CHAPTER I

THE INDIAN IMMIGRANT FAMILY

Since this book is a portrayal of the feelings and emotions of immigrants and their children, I am starting with a sketch of the Mehta family, a fictitious yet typical Indian-American family residing in the suburbs of a major American city.

BHARAT

At 50, Bharat Mehta is the head of this family. He is a medical doctor who received special training in cardiology in the United States. He has been in this country for 26 years. He comes from a middle class background in India and has two brothers and one sister, all of whom still reside in India. In his early years as a student in the United States, Bharat was amazed by the technology and advancement of American medical science. He was also amazed by the openness and advancement of American women. Despite an occasional dinner date with a classmate or acquaintance, he always knew that he wanted to go back to India to marry an Indian woman, a woman who would be best fit to be the mother of his children. After finishing his specialization, he returned to India to marry Usha, his wife now of 24 years.

After marriage, he was determined to come back to the United States, despite the urging of his parents. His mother, especially, dreaded the thought of her favorite, brightest son living so far away in "Uhm-ree-cah." He told them that he only planned to stay a short time, make some money, and then come back. He had big plans. He was going to buy his parents the new refrigerator and car they had always wanted.

A few months became a few years, and Bharat and his wife became acclimated to their lives in the States. Going back to India became less and less of an attractive prospect, the chances incrementally decreasing as each of their three children was born. Their lifestyles in the United States became almost a matter of habit, a habit that would be extremely trying to break.

Professionally, Bharat, like most of his Indian peers who immigrated in the 1960s, has excelled. He has operated his own medical practice for over 15 years and, in addition, has made several prudent investments in real estate and the stock market. Nonetheless, in the medical profession, Bharat has always felt a certain amount of discrimination, albeit subtle. While he was working for a medical group, there were times when he was certain that he was being passed up for a promotion or was not given a referral only because of his foreign background. He maintains that "in a foreign country, one is always treated like a second-class citizen."

Bharat and Usha have a group of Indian friends who reside in the same neighborhood, and they all regularly get together for parties on the weekends. Bharat plays tennis with some of these friends, and once a month the Indian men in the area meet in a local park to play cricket. Although he and Usha maintain good relations with his colleagues, he spends his work week looking forward to time he will spend with his Indian friends, speaking his native language and talking about Indian affairs.

He considers himself close to his children and makes it a point to attend all their school functions and other activities.

From the time they were born, Bharat and Usha have made the education of their children the highest priority. Bharat believes that it is important for an individual to be able to stand on his own feet, regardless of what his parents may be able to provide for him. He wants his children to realize the value of the opportunities they have before them and make use of them. He observes that Indian children in the States are very quick to assert their rights and ask for independence. He feels that they are rarely, however, willing to take on all the responsibilities that come along with independence and freedom. "Indian-American children," he says, "have a double standard of their own."

Lately, he has begun to worry a great deal about his oldest daughter, Shilpa's, marriage. To him, infatuation and love are on one side and compatibility and stability are on another. He believes that long-term compatibility for his daughter could best be found with a stable, educated Indian boy from a good family. As much as he hates to admit it, his daughter will not truly be her own person in his and in Indian society's eyes until she is married.

Bharat's own aging parents in India are another deep and painful concern to him. He has tried to bring them to the States to reside with his family several times, but they cannot adjust to life in this country. He feels as if he has somehow failed in the most important of functions for Indian sons—the duty to care for his parents, especially in their old age.

Bharat is proud of what he has accomplished in the United States and feels blessed to have three healthy and bright children. Nevertheless, in his view, their future in the States is unknown and ominous. As an immigrant, he feels that insecurity is akin to a scarlet letter "I" that one must wear on one's chest. "One never knows when people will get so jealous of us that they will want to throw us out," he says. More and more often, he thinks to himself, "This country is a *manhoos* [inauspicious] place."

Usha

Everyone who meets Usha is amazed to hear that she is now no less than 45 years old, for she appears much younger. She is striking in both Western and Indian attire. The only daughter among four sons of a middle class family, Usha was coddled by her extended family of grandparents, aunts, and uncles. She has fond memories of her childhood and her convent education. She returns to India often, in recent years accompanied only by her youngest son.

Usha was introduced to Bharat by "Ramu Kaka," a close friend of her father's and a distant relative of Bharat's mother. All she knew of Bharat when she first met him was that he had been a "topper" in medical college in India. The word "brilliant" was used often by various people to describe him. On their first meeting without their parents, Bharat and Usha went to see a Hindi film accompanied by Usha's older brother and his wife. Usha had never been alone with any man to whom she was not related. Usha decided to marry Bharat within two weeks of meeting him because he was "nice" and her father liked him. Besides, Bharat had to get back to the States, so a decision about the marriage had to be made quickly. A visa was arranged and off Usha went with a man she had known for two weeks to a country she had only read about in novels.

After a year, Usha grew accustomed to the novelty of being married. Around that time, a deep, sinking feeling began to gnaw at Usha regularly. She never called it homesickness, for that would be trivializing the emotions she was feeling. She describes it as an unsettling, almost nauseating sensation that struck her hardest in the evenings. Homesickness, she decided, was for those who missed their home, a home they felt was still theirs. What Usha felt was a realization that even her husband did not accept until many years later. Usha understood that she and Bharat were going to make this land of plenty and opportunity their permanent home. She also saw that as their chances of returning to India were nil, their right to call India their "home" would soon be non-existent.

Gradually, however, Usha began to enjoy running her own household and her own life. One of the first and only white American friends she made was an elderly lady who lived across the street. The woman took an immense liking to Usha and helped her purchase her first western-style dress at Sears. Usha had completed a master's degree in history in India and found satisfaction as a pre-school teacher, a job she continued to hold even when her salary was not needed to help the family financially.

Usha says that she lives for her children. She explains, "That's the way we Indians are—our families are our strength." She has always made sure that the children attended Indian parties and got involved in local Indian youth organizations in order to meet other Indian children. Lessons in Hindi and classical Indian dance along with regular trips to India were as routine for her children as piano, tennis lessons, and summer camp.

American society scares Usha. She watches "Oprah" and "Donahue" on television when the children are present and makes a concerted effort to express liberal attitudes on abortion and other such issues. Truthfully, she is simply pretending in order to keep the peace. Pre-marital sex, drug and alcohol abuse, and her perception of general American promiscuity frighten her. She would not dare express her true feelings for fear of an uprise from her children. She feels that all three of the children are easily agitated by her and her "old-fashioned, Indian outlook." Usha is especially proud of her daughter Shilpa, but her fierce independence leaves Usha frustrated. Usha repeatedly asks Shilpa in their many heated arguments, "Why be so set in your ways? Why not accept the advice of people who have experienced life?"

Usha is frightened, and she admits it. For her and Bharat, the children are all they have in an alien nation. If she loses them to the dark forces of American society, she does not know where she would go. "Why do our children act so American?" she asks Bharat.

Children in America grow up so fast, Usha feels. Of course, she wants everything for them. Though she frequently indulges her children, she often feels that they see her as an opposing force, rather than as someone on their side. She is almost saddened by her children's level of worldliness and maturity. At the same time, although she admits it to no one, she is also intimidated by it.

SHILPA

The Mehta's first-born, Shilpa, just celebrated her twenty-third birthday at which Bharat and Usha, despite Shilpa's resistance, threw a party inviting 100 of their closest friends. It was a grand affair, catered by the finest Indian restaurant in town and featuring a D.J. who played a mix of American dance music with Indian "Disco Bhangra." The Mehtas' family friends marveled at how "balanced, sensible, and mature" Shilpa is and how she is a role model for younger Indian children. A chorus of guffaws arose from the group as they also suggested that Bharat and Usha start looking for a boy for Shilpa to marry. Little did the unsuspecting and well-meaning group of "Aunties" and "Uncles" realize that for all her apparent good sense and maturity, Shilpa often feels utterly confused, naive, and directionless. Would it be right to allow her parents to be involved in the choosing of her spouse? How would her American friends react to that? On the other hand, does she have the gumption and self-reliance of her American friends to find her own mate through years of dating?

Shilpa grew up believing that her mother wished that her first-born was a son. Shilpa admits that this feeling has instilled in her a definite "female, Indian angst" that causes some of her mother's friends and indeed, some of her own peer group, to perceive her as something of an Indian bra-burning feminist. She firmly asserts, though, that she believes in all of the positive ideals of the traditional Indian woman, including duty to family and loyalty and fidelity to one's spouse. Nevertheless, her personal ideal is to live life without limits. When the Indian vision of a traditional female becomes limiting, she becomes frustrated.

Shilpa is academically bright and did well in her first year of law school. She feels that most of the satisfaction of her accomplishments has come from watching her parents take such immense pride in her. Her love for her parents and siblings is deep and "intertwined in her gut," she says.

Nevertheless, as she gets older, she feels that communication within the family is on the surface only. She feels that her parents only want to hear the good news but not the bad; they want to share in her triumphs and successes but not in her doubts and insecurities and sadness. Major problems are always swept under the rug. "You are smart. You will figure out a way," is her father's classic response when she starts to share a problem with him. She envies her white American friends who seemingly can tell their parents, their mothers especially, virtually anything.

Shilpa's exasperation with her mother has resulted in regular arguments within the past few years. Shilpa feels that her mother simply "switches off" when she tries to share her feelings with her. "She just walks away or pretends to be involved in a television show or something when I talk to her," Shilpa says. Shilpa thinks that if there were a little picture in the dictionary by the word "indifferent," it would be a picture of Usha Mehta. In her attempts to psychoanalyze the situation (a favorite hobby of Shilpa's), she decided that her mother takes all the frustrations of being an immigrant out on her first-born. Shilpa feels that Usha pushes her too hard, chastizing her on every possible occasion and then not providing the encouragement or support she needs to accomplish the things she pushes her to do.

Shilpa wishes she could share her enthusiasm for life and her goals and aspirations with her mother, but she believes that all she would get in return would be a pessimistic remark about the "badness" of American society. Shilpa is bright and charming. Her parents' friends adore her and say how they wish their own daughters could be more like her. "How ironic," Shilpa once said to a friend, "that the whole world could love me, but my own mother is disgusted by me."

Recently, she has been seeing an American man whom she met in college. Her parents are not aware of their relationship, and she lies to them in order to see him. She is torn. On the one hand, she feels justified in protecting her parents from something they would be hurt to know and, for that matter, from something that they would absolutely not accept. On the other hand, it pains her to hide something so important in her life from her parents. "Whose fault do you think it is that I feel so compelled to hide this from my parents?" she says. "Why am I so different? What makes me so special? Why don't I have a right to do this?"

DINESH

When Dinesh Mehta was born nineteen years ago, Usha was thrilled at giving birth to the son she and Bharat had always wanted. Dinesh would contend, however, that he is nowhere near the son his parents would like to have had. He is by no means a star student like his sister, but he tries his best. He is asked by his parents' friends at Indian parties if he would like to go into the "may-dee-cul" profession and become a brilliant doctor like his father. If not medicine, then perhaps he would like to study engineering or computers, the Aunties and Uncles suggest. "None of the above" is the answer Dinesh curtly gives them all. He is fascinated by government and politics and would like to have a career in policymaking. "You could never do it," his father told him upon hearing of his son's career goals. "You are used to such luxury and comforts. You will come crying back to us when you find that you can't even feed yourself on a government clerk's wages."

During high school, Dinesh shunned everything even remotely related to India. His idea of weekend fun did not include spending time with "nerdy" Indian kids. He wanted to be just like his American friends at school. Since he left for college two years ago, however, Dinesh has begun to wear his "Indianness" on his sleeve. "Being different is cool," he says. He gladly volunteers to explain the difference between Mahatma and Indira Gandhi as well as the sacredness of the cow and the structure of the Hindu caste system to his peers and professors. During his freshman year, he even began associating strictly with other Indian college students whom he met through the university's India Club. He enjoyed learning Indian folk dances and how to make *samosas* with other Indian young people, and he discovered that Indian girls weren't so bad after all. But when he heard one white American student derogatorily call the India Club members "a bunch of camel jockeys," he began widening his circle of friends to include people in other ethnic groups. Hanging around exclusively with other Indians would make him exactly like his parents, and this disturbed him. "Balance is key," he decided.

Dinesh is dating a Filipino girl, and his parents are fully aware of their relationship. Bharat and Usha are not thrilled by the idea, but Dinesh has assured them that the relationship is not serious ("It's just for fun, a casual thing," he says) and that he fully intends to marry an Indian girl. Dinesh's parents warn him about American girls (his parents define "American" as anything or anyone that did not originate in India) who try to get their "hooks" into Indian boys because they are smart and ambitious and will always remain faithful. Whenever his parents hear of an American woman marrying an Indian man, they remark with remorse, "*Phasadia, bechare ko*" [she ensnared the poor man].

Dinesh identifies strongly with the hardships his parents faced and continue to face as immigrants. Although he sometimes chides his father for repeating his stories of coming to this country with only a few dollars to his name, Dinesh actually feels a great deal of pride in their achievements. He does not understand, though, how such educated, accomplished people could be so closed-minded on so many issues. AIDS, a high divorce rate, drug abuse, and violent crime in the United States are all elements Bharat and Usha point to as evidence of a lack of values and morals in the American system. Dinesh has stopped expressing an alternate opinion on these subjects because when he does, his parents feel that he is simply trying to start an argument. "It's like they only see the bad, not the good in the U.S.," says Dinesh. "They give this place a bad rap." Dinesh disagrees with but ultimately accedes to his parents' viewpoint. "I guess it is easier for me to see where they are coming from, but harder for them to understand why I think the way I do," he says.

ARUN

At age 13, Arun is the youngest of the Mehta brood. Lately, he is the only one of the Mehta children who continues the regular visits to India. He has never minded because he has cousins there of his age and, frankly, he enjoys the attention they shower on their relative from "States."

Arun, who lets his friends call him "Aaron" instead of insisting that they use the correct Hindi pronunciation, "Uh-roon," became conscious of his ethnic background in the first grade when one of his classmates called him "a little brown cookie." Bharat and Usha mistakenly assume that confusion over being Indian and American starts during the teenage years and not before. Arun, however, started to make some decisions, both positive and negative, about what it means to be Indian even at age seven.

Lately, he seems a bit befuddled by Hinduism. He hears terms like "Hairy Krishnas" and "voodoo Hindus" on television and in the movies and wonders if he should take it personally. He also cannot figure out whether or not to feel offended by the numerous parodies of Indian drugstore clerks he sees in the media. He says that he is not really sure if he has a right to be offended. "My parents don't seem to mind when people say things against Indians, so why should I?" he says.

Arun's father often emphasizes the greatness of India and Indian culture. "Dad says a lot of neat things about our motherland," says Arun. But recently, Arun asked his parents, "If India is so great, why are we here?" Even at his age, he could tell that his parents were both confounded and hurt by the poignancy of their son's question. He did not see that his parents were also struggling with that same question. Arun did not get an answer, and he never asked the question again.

That the feelings and development of each individual are important to other members of the family is clear. Each member of the family admits to feeling an intense, almost visceral love for the others. Nevertheless, the attitudes and actions of the adults and children are often misperceived and misconstrued in the midst of the deep-set insecurity that each one of the Mehtas feels.

The Mehtas' concerns may not be drastically different from those of other professional families in a post-industrial society. Yet for immigrants and their children, normal and expected family tensions are compounded by the fact that these families maintain an almost schizophrenic existence, attempting to straddle two different and strong cultures. For the children, ever since their early years, right and wrong and good and bad are all tangled in a vague definition of what is Indian and what is American. "Values" and "culture" have become tiresome words for them, concepts that have received too much family airtime in their lives. For the parents, the goals of education and professional success of their early adulthood have been achieved. They fear having to watch their children's and indeed their own sense of values and ideals whisked away by the forces of a still alien country that is not under their control.

Indian immigrants and their children are forging new identities—Indian-American identities—seeking a sense of culture without caste, custom, or ritual. Like sculptors, they are attempting to create a sense of themselves from "scratch." They are inexperienced, almost unwilling craftsmen. Like artists subscribing to two different schools of thought, each generation maintains different ideas of what the end product should be. In the process of creating these identities, these different artists are likely to find that their renderings are not identical. Each generation's final work of art, however, may have some common characteristics, each sculpture influenced and shaped by the other, resulting in pieces that are beautiful in their diversity.

This book attempts to describe and explain the condition of post-1965 professional Indian immigrant families in the United States. The information presented herein is based on reported facts, meaning it is based on what these families themselves articulated as their concerns. To some readers, some of the findings may be perceived as negative. Nevertheless, the very fact that this community is wrestling with the issues of identity illustrates that they have something at stake. If reconciling a dual identity was an easier process for this group, perhaps it would indicate that they had totally adopted one culture over the other. The challenge lies in balancing both cultures and in these families' commitment to achieving such a balance.

I eat what you tell me, I swallow my pride...
I've come a long way from home...
Yes, I've changed my look and I've changed my walk...
I mind my manners and I know how to talk...
Yes, you've changed me but you know I'm gonna change you...
— *Nobuko Miyamoto, "Ballad"*

(in Making Waves: An Anthology of Writings By and
About Asian American Women)

CHAPTER II

THE IMMIGRANT STORY

BACKGROUND

A fundamental premise of this study is that Indian immigrants who came to this country in the wake of the 1965 Immigration Act are different from a majority of other immigrant groups in several ways. Most notably, this group possesses a surprisingly high educational level and concentration in the professional fields. According to the *1980 Census Asian and Pacific Islander Report*, among Indians in the United States, the highest percentage were employed in "managerial and professional specialty occupations." Consequently, the median household income for Indians at that time was reported as $25,644—in contrast to $18,544 for Chinese immigrant households and $16,841 for all U.S. households.

Another element that makes Indians distinct from other immigrants is the profound diversity within the immigrant group. Seven major religions, thirty-three major languages, thousands of dialects, and six primary regional classifications characterize the Indian population. The immigrants reflect this diversity. Gujus, Punjus, Bongos, and Marus (slang terms for individuals of different regional backgrounds in India) abound in the United States, as do other Indian cultural groups. As one immigrant explained, "Saying that you are from India is like saying that you are from Europe—India is a huge, diverse place, and it is often not enough of a common bond to bring immigrants together."

As compared to other recent immigrant groups, especially Chinese, Koreans, and other Asians, the Indians have a very high level of English proficiency. East Asian community leaders, in fact, observe that English proficiency is an advantage that Indians have over other Asians. As a remnant of British colonial rule, most schools in India maintain English as a primary language beginning at very early levels. All of the interviews conducted for this study, for instance, were done in English, reflecting the comfort level most immigrants feel with the English language. Finally, physically Indians are what some would call "dark Caucasians," often passing for other ethnic backgrounds, including Hispanic or Middle Eastern.[1]

Sociologist Nathan Glazer summarized the atypical nature of Indian immigrants by describing them as "...a new and rapidly growing ethnic group fed by immigration. It is not like any of the other[s]. It is marked off by a high level of education, by concentration in the professions, by a strong commitment to maintaining family connections, both here in the United States and in India".[2]

REASONS FOR IMMIGRATION TO THE UNITED STATES

Why did so many professional people of Indian origin choose to immigrate to the United States after 1965? The nature of the 1965 Immigration Act provides an explanation of why the United States was attractive, as well as why the immigrant population included such highly educated people. The 1960s saw a surge toward technological modernization in the United States and a shortage of people to staff this development. As a result, the Act gave professionals and other skilled laborers

[1] *Takaki, p. 295*
[2] *Saran, p. 25*

high priority. Most Indians originally immigrated on student visas to seek postgraduate degrees in technical and scientific areas, having already completed undergraduate education in India. According to sociologist Parmatma Saran, "The very nature of the immigration law is such that only members of certain professional backgrounds and educational qualifications were granteu immigrant visas...An overwhelming majority of Indian immigrants possess high educational qualifications. The largest number of them are engineers and doctors. Others are college teachers and scientific researchers".[3] Recalled one man who obtained a visa because of his electrical engineering background, "Immigration policy was definitely selective. [American companies thought] if they could get an already trained person from abroad, why spend the money training them?"

Among the sample of interviewees, the predominant reasons for immigrating were the educational, professional and, economic opportunities the United States seemed to offer. Much of this is related to the images they had of the United States while they were still in India. Said Amit, 53, an engineering consultant with his own business, "All we knew of America was what we saw in Western movies and read in novels. To us, there was abundance galore. It seemed like the streets were paved with gold."

Specifically, many saw opportunities greater than those available to them in India. In other words, one should separately analyze the pull of America and the push from India to immigrate. Said Sumeet, 45, a software engineer, "In India, there are too many people competing for few openings in top universities. Nepotism and bribery make it difficult for someone to get anywhere purely on merit. There, you run to stand still." Fiction writer Bharati Mukherjee captures this feeling in her short story "A Father," which centers around an Indian professional and his family settled in the Midwest, "All through his teenage years, Mr. Bhowmick had dreamed of success abroad. What form that success would take he had left vague.

[3] *Saran, p. 100*

Success had meant to him escape from the constant plotting and bitterness that wore out India's middle class".[4]

A comparison of salaries in India and the United States further explains the economic motives for immigration. In India, a doctor in a private hospital would make about $6,000 per year, compared to an average yearly salary of about $71,000 in the U.S. Similarly, a managing engineer would earn approximately $3,600 per annum in India compared to $41,991 in this country, and a university professor would make $3,000 yearly compared to the $39,900 of his American counterpart.[5] Although one must consider the relative buying power of Indian versus American wages, when Indians considered the potential conversion of U.S. salaries into Indian currency, the idea of immigrating became highly attractive.

Interestingly, more than half of the sample's original intention was either to obtain education in the United States and then return to India or to work for a few years, gather a substantial amount of money, and go back. Said Asha, 46, homemaker and mother of three, "My husband and I thought that he would complete his Ph.D., work for a few years, then we could return to India with a lot of money. Somehow, a few years became twenty-two years. We had children, got caught up in life here, and didn't go back." Indian immigrants may have tried to soften the psychological blow of leaving their country by defining the move as temporary, not permanent.

THE IMMIGRANT EXPERIENCE

Despite glamorous preconceptions of the United States before arriving, most immigrants endured difficulties upon arriving in this country, both professional and psychological.

Although Indian immigrants were skilled professionally and generally did not take jobs as menial or blue-collar laborers upon their arrival, many said they faced hardships in the work place. Said Ashok, 51, general practitioner, "Getting a visa was just the first step. We had to spend the first several years proving ourselves. Our accents were different. Our ways of working

[4] *Mukherjee, p. 65*
[5] *Helweg, p. 251*

were different. The physicians among us initially got jobs in the worst neighborhoods and then gradually did better."

In terms of the psychological adjustment, many commented that they missed the support of extended family and found the pace of life in the United States to be incredibly fast. Said Surjit, 48, a mechanical engineer, "In this country, you are always trying to catch up. There is no *santosh* [Hindi word for satisfaction or mental peace]. In India, one enjoys life. Time spent with the family or friends often takes priority over mundane, every-day work routine." Added Vikas, 48, "Life here is so lonely. Everyone is so alone. This loneliness is common in America. In India, I would be living in a joint family with my parents and siblings and nieces and nephews. I would be friendly with all the people in my neighborhood. This is not the case here."

The women interviewed, especially, said that their images of the United States prior to immigrating were not consistent with the actualities of life in the United States. Said Uma, 42, "Life isn't a disco in the States. As immigrants, we had little support when we first arrived—few friends, no money, no family." It seems that women, especially, felt the loss of family and friends more than men. Said Neera, 44, "My husband used to go to work all day. I was left all day in the home. I longed to talk to someone in Hindi or see someone in Indian clothes. On weekends, we would go to the airport just to look for other Indian people."

Female Indian immigrants came to the United States almost exclusively because of their husbands' opportunities for career advancement. Even the first generation women who had professional degrees said that they came to the United States because of their husbands' decisions to do so. Thus, the female immigrants' reactions to the United States were quite different from those of the men. One immigrant woman, for instance, explained that it took her several years before she was comfortable speaking with and interacting with white Americans. She felt that the process of adjustment was much easier for her husband, as he interacted with white Americans at the university and later at work. In many instances, the women were more inclined than the men to associate strictly with other Indians.

DEMOGRAPHICS

Official demographic information on the Indian immigrant population is limited to the statistics provided by the 1980 Census, which indicated 361,544 individuals of Indian origin residing in the United States. A 1987 Government of India study, on the other hand, showed 525,600 individuals of Indian origin residing in the States.[6] Demographers of ethnic communities emphasize that from the 1980 figures, one may extrapolate that many more people of Indian origin, both legal and illegal immigrants, have made their home in this country. A recent *Wall Street Journal* article, in fact, predicted that the 1990 Census results may show over 900,000 individuals of Indian origin residing in the U.S.[7]

Already, the first of the 1990 Census figures show that the Asian population has more than doubled in the United States since 1980. In fact, in the state of California alone, 1990 Census data indicate that Indians had the second largest percentage increase in population among all Asian groups. The figures show 159,973 Indians residing in California, an increase of 176.3% since 1980.[8] As further data becomes available, one may expect evidence of a similar Indian population increase in other parts of the country.

Asian Indians in the United States are presently concentrated in the following states: California, New York, Illinois, New Jersey, and Texas. A majority of immigrants apparently chose to settle in the major metropolitan areas within these states, such as New York City, Los Angeles, the San Francisco Bay Area, Chicago, and Houston, as jobs were most available in these locations. College towns are also home to a number of Indian immigrants, again due to job availability. A surprisingly high number, however, also reside in smaller cities throughout the country. For instance, locations as unlikely as Aberdeen,

[6] *Helweg, p. 240*
[7] WSJ, *1/27/89*
[8] India West, *5/17/91*

South Dakota and Norman, Oklahoma have Indian communities. Indians abroad often cite a comic phrase that roughly translated says, "Indians reach the places where even the sun's rays do not reach."

CHARACTERISTICS

In their own words, the immigrants interviewed for this study described themselves as extremely hardworking, determined to succeed, aggressive, risk-taking, money-minded, family-oriented, and yet individualistic with respect to contributing to both the Indian and non-Indian communities in general. According to several Indian community leaders, the extent of their professional success surpasses those of any other recent immigrant community. Said National Federation of Indian-American Associations President Inder Singh at a gathering of Indian professionals, "Our professors have earned national and international claim. Our scholars and intellectuals have published numerous books. Our entrepreneurs who came to this country with less than $50 are now multi-millionaires."

There are a variety of reasons for why this group attained such high levels of professional success in such a short time. Those interviewed concurred that the very makeup of the immigrant population rendered them likely to achieve in this country. The individuals who came to the U.S. represented the "cream of the crop" with respect to education in India. A majority completed their undergraduate educations in the top Indian technological and scientific institutes. As one man put it, "What was a 'brain drain' for India was a 'brain gain' for the United States." Furthermore, having given up the relatively secure prospects that education from a top school affords people in India, the immigrants were exceptionally motivated to succeed. In essence, they had "five dollars in their pockets, and a million dollars between their ears."

Despite a relatively rapid rise to high socio-economic levels in their new country, the Indian immigrants' civic, social, and community activity, for the most part, remains limited to other Indians. Over 80% of the sample reported that aside from an occasional gathering with colleagues, their social associations were with other Indians only. Said Seema, 39, "I find that American women are much different in their values, much more advanced sexually. I feel comfortable with other Indian women of similar backgrounds." Indian families residing in the same area form "cliques" of sorts and regularly have parties or get-togethers on the weekends. Often referred to as "ISG's" or "Indian Social Gatherings," these parties seem universal to Indian communities throughout the country and have become an institution of sorts. The apparent parochiality of the community is understandable, according to one recent study of Asian Indian immigrants:

> Among their own, the immigrants have different behavioral characteristics. They are free to shout or sing, laugh or cry. Even their English accent is different. Among Westerners, they are superb imitators and behave properly, tell the right jokes, laugh at the correct time and assume the correct posture, but the smiles are not as wide, the laughter not as loud, and the hug not as hard as when they are among Indians.[9]

In addition to their attachments to Indians abroad, the immigrants continue to maintain strong ties to India. Given that this group of immigrants came to the States beginning in the mid 1960s, many have now spent more years of their lives living abroad than they have spent living in India. Yet, the bonds with India seem unrelentingly strong. Many still have extended families living in India. *One hundred percent* of the adult sample had visited India with their spouses and children at least once since immigration. Interest in Indian politics and affairs, documented by numerous publications for Indians in the United States, is strong, as reflected by the knowledge level of the sample. Although no one in the sample had acted on their original intentions of returning permanently to India within a few years, over 70% said they had entertained the idea of ultimately settling in India. Only one person, however, said that he was definite in his intentions to return.

[9] *Helweg, p. 127*

With respect to their backgrounds in India, most come from middle class socio-economic status. Parents of immigrants were often professionals themselves; it is clear that very few of the upper class or lower class were either interested in or able to immigrate. The vast majority is Hindu, with high concentrations from the Indian states of Punjab and Gujarat. In addition to Hindus, there are minor concentrations of Muslims, Sikhs, and Christians. There is no accurate way to describe the immigrant population in terms of caste. It seems that caste has become a second consideration for immigrants behind regional background. In general, the immigrants are reflective of India's regional and religious diversity.

CROSSROADS: WHAT NEXT?

Based on the results of this study, an argument explaining the direction in which the Indian-American community is headed can be made as follows: Indian immigrants achieved an unusually high level of success in the approximately 25 years they have resided in the United States. Their rise to the higher socio-economic levels of American society, coupled with the fact that they are not, for the most part, involved in other spheres of American life, namely, social, civic, and political, poses certain issues for the community. The most pressing of these issues seems to be the question of what will happen to the next generation, the children of these immigrants, most of whom were either born or spent their formative years in the United States.

One may conclude that the community of post-1965 Indian immigrants is at a crossroads. Having achieved their professional goals, they are concerned about their future, specifically the future of their children. Said Inder, 52, an electrical engineer, "You may ask us any questions about politics, discrimination, civil rights, job[s], but what we immigrants care about most is what will become of our children. Will they keep their Indian culture?" Added Shanti, 44, "Do I care more about putting an Indian in Congress or finding a suitable Indian boy for my daughter [to marry]? I obviously care more about my own children." While economic well-being was the primary concern for immigrants when they first arrived, as their children enter adulthood, the focus of this community is on the second generation.

Mera jootha hai Japani,
Yeh pathloon Inglistani,
Sar peh lal topi Rusi,
Phir bhi dil hai Hindustani.

My shoes are Japanese,
My trousers are English,
The hat on my head is Russian,
But, still my heart is Indian.
                    —Song from Hindi film 'Shree 420'

CHAPTER III

THE SECOND GENERATION

BACKGROUND

From the interviews, both with the random sample as well as with community leaders, as well as from conferences, forums, and publications aimed at Indians in the U.S., it is clear that the adaptation and future of the second generation is a primary issue for the immigrant community. Individuals in the first generation sample concur that at the time of immigration, they gave very little thought to how their children would cope with balancing their Indian backgrounds with their American up-bringing. Similarly, most of the second generation sample asserted that they are somewhat unprepared to face the problems of dual culturalism, as they had little voice in their parents' decision to immigrate. Said Mona, 21, "I did not ask to be born here. When my parents first decided to come here, I don't think they stopped to think about how their kids would develop."

The post-1965 immigrants have spent an average of 15 to 25 years in this country, and the approximate age span of their offspring is from 12 to 25 years. The future of children apparently became a concern beginning in the mid-1970s when they began entering "impressionable ages".[1]

Said Madhu, 48, mother of two, "I like it when my kids learn initiative and hard work and other things that are important in American culture. But I don't like it when they question me on everything and keep repeating like robots, 'I don't care. I don't care.' We want them to know about Indian culture and not become totally American. There seems to be no respect for elders or experience in this country." To address some of these concerns, groups of parents have organized classes in traditional language, dance, and culture to educate the second generation.

Parents make their investment for the future through their progeny. Consequently, many immigrant families put great amounts of time and money into the upbringing of their children. Said Kumar, 49, "I will sacrifice to make sure my children never lack in anything—education, material things, anything. They should have the best of everything." It is essential to realize how important, emotionally and psychologically, it is for immigrant parents to ensure the future success and well-being of their children,

> An Indian's home is a compartment where one has to face whether life is meaningful, which for most Indians is largely determined by their children. When this domestic realm is invaded by contradictory values and beliefs, the very core of an Indian's self-worth is challenged.[2]

The situations and abilities of immigrant parents change over time. When children are young, parents devote a great deal of their time and energy toward "making it" in this country. During the initial years, the idea of balancing quality time with the family and time spent at work may not be feasible for immigrants, as they are looking not solely to survive but to make their fortune. During this time it is often the mother who is closely involved in child-rearing. If the mother is not herself employed, it is probable that her interaction with others is

[1] *Helweg, p. 115*
[2] *Helweg, p. 138*

32

limited primarily to other Indians. Many immigrants, for instance, went back to India to have arranged marriages and then returned to the States. In many cases, the mother may not have been in this country for very long. Her ability to impart knowledge of American ways is limited.

As the children get older, parents find themselves comfronting social forces (such as dating, peer pressure, alcohol, drugs, and pre-marital sex) that are completely alien to them. Their insecurity in a foreign land is compounded by the fact that they feel they are losing control of their children. After having achieved all the economic and professional success that they originally sought, they are almost panic-stricken with respect to the future of their children. It is important, therefore, to remain sensitive to the emotions and limitations of immigrant parents.

Nevertheless, from the point of view of the second generation, the question of identity seems to override many other concerns.

COCONUTS: BROWN ON THE OUTSIDE, WHITE ON THE INSIDE

The confusion that stems from attempting to balance traditional, Indian values with all things "American" faced outside the home is a prevalent issue among Indian-American youth. A significant finding of this study is that this process of reconciling identity does not begin or end at a particular age. Of course, individuals face this question in varying degrees at different stages in their lives. The point is, however, that wrestling with identity is not a "phase." Developing positive or negative ideas about one's Indian background begins at a young age and may continue throughout adulthood. This factor is important to consider, especially since, as discussed earlier, many children's upbringing remains highly traditional in the early years due to parental unfamiliarity with American ways.

The identity crisis that many Indian youth face has been termed the "American-Born Confused *Desi*" or "ABCD" complex. The word *desi* means "native" or "countryman." The phrase is mocking, yet poignantly accurate. Interestingly, Indians in India coined this term to describe their American counterparts.

College student Vindu Goel expressed this sense of cultural confusion in a magazine for Indian-Americans:

> Who are your heroes supposed to be, George Washington and Abraham Lincoln, or Akbar the Great and Mahatma Gandhi? Sitting in history class, you identify with the American colonists fighting for independence in 1776. Then you realize that your ancestors had nothing to do with it. You feel terrible about the way 'we Americans' enslaved the blacks. But 'you' didn't do it; in fact, your ancestors were busy being mistreated by the British in Asia. Which nation's past is your own? You don't know.[3]

In a story about an Indian-American family, Bharati Mukherjee further captures the predicament of many second generation Indians, "Girls like Babli were caught between the rules...They were too smart, too impulsive for a backward place like Ranchi, but not tough enough nor smart enough for sex-crazy places like Detroit".[4]

The Indian young people interviewed, without exception, expressed that they have been challenged by the attempt to reconcile their identities as both Indians and Americans. As Gauri, 22, put it, "We are coconuts—brown on the outside, white on the inside." The situation of second generation Indian-Americans is distinct from that of Indian immigrants in other nations. American society is relatively absorbent in nature; social barriers are not highly prevalent, and children of ethnic backgrounds are able to adopt American social norms. In contrast, the substantial Indian population in Kenya does not mix with the native population; thus, over three generations later, young Indians still strongly adhere to traditional ways, almost as if they never left India. In England, similarly, Indians are considered "colored" in certain social strata and not as readily accepted.

This situation in which second generation Indians attempt to be both Indian and American results in what anthropologists

---

[3] Awaaz, *1988*
[4] *Mukherjee, p. 72*

Arthur W. and Usha M. Helweg label "compartmentalization"; in other words, the children of immigrants "compartmentalize their lives, living at home according to parental dictates and at school according to the culture of their friends".[5] The extent to which this is psychologically unhealthy for the second generation is a point of concern for both generations.

WALKING A TIGHTROPE: DIFFERENCES IN CULTURE

Another major reason why young Indian-Americans find it so difficult to balance both the Indian and American cultures is that there are such fundamental differences between the two. In fact, the cultures come into direct conflict over a number of issues. With respect to family structure, Indians traditionally believe in generations of one family residing together in a "joint family"; the system is hierarchical based on seniority. The concept of Western individualism and more equality in the family structure is foreign. Age is respected in the Indian structure, and elders are considered the leaders of the family. On the other hand, one might argue that a "cult of youth" prevails in Western culture; youth is exalted and celebrated, and old age is mocked and denigrated.

The Indian parent-child relationship, furthermore, is highly authoritarian. In her paper for an Indian-American conference on family and youth, Dr. Nalini Juthani explained that in Indian culture, "Open expression of opposition is discouraged. Communication is not open if it is disrespectful. 'The wounds of physical abuse will heal, but the wounds caused by words will not heal' is a well-known Indian saying." In Western culture, children are encouraged to be more "why-oriented"; questioning authority is seen as a sign of independence and intellectual development. Juthani argues that in American society "open communication with expression of anger is acceptable. 'Sticks and stones will break my bones, but words will never hurt me' is a totally opposite saying [compared to the Indian outlook]."

Similar differences in culture are encountered by other immigrant groups, especially Asian communities. For instance,

[5] *Helweg, p. 181*

the first generation Japanese or *Nisei* experienced concern over the seemingly conflicting values of dating, marriage, and other social issues that their children or *Issei* learned in school.[6] Other immigrant groups, such as the Koreans and the Chinese, who also came to this nation in the wake of the 1965 Immigration Act, express a desire for their children to retain traditional ways, despite these children's American upbringing.[7]

Nevertheless, the Indian situation is different from other Asian groups for a number of reasons. First, the Indian culture maintains a more severe taboo on openness in pre-marital, male-female relationships. Dating is not an institution in India, as marriages are traditionally arranged by one's family. Anyone, especially a female, who acquires a reputation of dating many people may have difficulty marrying into a respectable family. This taboo is rigid compared to most Asian groups. Many of the Indian youths interviewed said that most of their Asian friends were allowed to date, and many, in fact, dated other Asians. The Indian community faces an additional disadvantage in that their population in the U.S. is not large enough for them to associate strictly with other Indians. In other words, it is difficult for them to avoid contact with Western social pressures. Another way in which Indians differ from other Asians is in their inability to assimilate into American society on a religious level. Many Koreans, Chinese, and Japanese have adopted some form of Christianity over the generations. They meet and interact with other Americans through the church. In contrast, a majority of the Indian immigrants are Hindu, Muslim, or Sikh, and religious interaction with non-Indians is highly uncommon.

Finally, as most of the people in the second generation sample concurred, Indian parents raise their children according to the standards with which they, themselves, grew up in India over 25 years ago and are unaware of the increasing liberalization of social attitudes in India itself. Said Sita, 19, "All my cousins [in India] are allowed to date and go out. They get away with things that our parents would totally forbid us to do."

[6] *Sowell, p. 170*
[7] Peninsula News, *7/15/89*

Added Sumita, 44, an immigrant who knows several professional families in India, "It will greatly help the second generation to point out that the first generation has a static image of the India of their youth. Today, in professional families in India, the youngsters are allowed to go out freely, and 'love marriages' are becoming more common."

COLLEGE LIFE: "I AM INDIAN"

The struggle to reconcile two cultures is indeed prevalent in the lives of second generation Indians. Nevertheless, evidence indicates that this struggle subsides considerably once young Indian-Americans reach college age. In fact, among those 18 to 25-year-olds sampled, the overwhelming sense of affiliation was with their Indian background. Granted, all those youth born and raised in the United States have lost some degree of their "Indianness." Yet, when asked how they would identify themselves, 95% of the interviewees responded that they were Indian, without any qualifications. Moreover, 70% of those college students said that they had recently made efforts to familiarize themselves with their native language, either by speaking the language with their parents or by taking classes in college. Among their concerns was how to preserve the culture for future generations. Interestingly, the college-age students found younger Indian-Americans to be more rebellious and confused over their Indian heritage. Said Purvi, 21, "When I see Indian teenage girls wearing pounds of make-up, dressed like Madonna, drinking and partying, I wonder what kind of confusion is going on in their minds. I feel like they are compromising themselves because they are not sure of their identity."

Several factors explain why second generation Indians start to feel "back-to-India" sentiments once they reach the college level. The interviewees asserted that as they grew older they started to feel more comfortable with themselves and, therefore, felt a stronger affiliation with their Indian backgrounds. This increased affiliation is manifested in a number of ways. Many drop the Americanized versions of their names in favor of their given names. For example, Roger reverts to Raj, and

Michael metamorphosizes into Munjal. Higher concentrations of other Indian-American students also seems to encourage positive feelings toward one's Indian background. Most students said they were involved in the "India Clubs" at their universities and found that they enjoyed the company of other second generation Indian students. Said Aarti, 22, "When you go to college, you find other Indian students whose parents are the same way that yours are. You don't have to constantly explain things to them because they understand how you were brought up. Since coming to college, most of my friends and roommates have been Indian because I feel more comfortable with them."

Campus "India Clubs" are university-affiliated organizations designed to encourage interaction between students of Indian origin. Activities are both social and cultural; dances and parties as well as classical music performances and lectures on India appear on club agendas. Many of these clubs evolved to meet the needs of Indian students raised in the United States, needs that are often quite different from those of students who come directly from India. Said Mamta, 21, "The students straight from India want to talk about Indian politics and Indian affairs. We [Indian-Americans] don't know what they are talking about and would rather get to know each other and more about Indian culture." Added Mahendra, 19, "Students straight from India think we are totally ridiculous. They laugh at our American accents and think we don't care about India." In several instances, students directly from India and Indian-American students maintain separate organizations.

Representatives of the major "India Clubs" in the greater Los Angeles area all said that their groups have little to no interaction with other campus Asian clubs. Club leaders said that although Indians are "Asian" by geographical definition, there has been little mix between the Indian associations and the Chinese, Japanese, Korean, Thai, Vietnamese, and Filipino groups. Said one Indian student, "We [Indians and other Asians] may have similar characteristics, but we can't be lumped together with them." Another student added that Indians interact more with the Middle Eastern student groups. Said Raghu, 20, "You know you have something in common when people use the same racial slur to describe both groups. A lot of people call Indians and Middle Easterners 'camel jockeys.'"

Recently, groups have realized the need for young Indians to interact with one another, even outside of their individual universities. For instance, the San Francisco Bay Area-based Coalition of Indo-American Students (CIAS) was founded to "bring together students of Indian origin, so that we may share ideas, understand each other better, and rally around issues that are important to us," according to club president Dhruv Gupta.

The primary reason behind the increased affinity that these college students feel seems to relate to the way in which they are perceived by others once they are "on their own." In other words, beyond the home environment, young Indian-Americans feel that *others* identify them as Indians, regardless of the way they perceive themselves. Said Ankur Goel, 26, publisher of *Awaaz* magazine and author of several articles on second generation Indians, "In high school and college I wasn't involved with Indian groups. I didn't have many Indian friends. But as we enter graduate school or the working world, we start to see we are a bit different. Maybe American society was pointing out to us that we are different".[8] Some young Indian-Americans often experience a shocking realization of their ethnicity. For instance, one young woman who was born, raised, and educated in the United States related the story of her interview with a prestigious law firm. Despite her impressive background and Ivy League degree, the interviewer repeatedly asked her questions about where she was born and her citizenship status. "The man did not see my degree or my qualifications. All he saw was a little, brown woman," she explained. "It was strange for me to be identified as a foreigner when all the while I thought I was as American as anyone else." One might infer that this heightened sense of being different leads to a greater acceptance of ethnic background.

[8] India Today, *8/31/89*

British-Indian writer Hanif Kureishi summarized the process of coming to terms with ethnic identity,

> You always know who you are until people ask you about it...I always felt I was an English boy until people said to me, 'Do you really belong here?' Or, 'Do you feel at home in England?' So your identity doesn't get shaken until other people doubt it. One's identity has to be some sort of alliance between the way you see yourself and the way other people in the world see you.[9]

The impulse for many Indian-Americans at the college level seems to be toward understanding and sharing this "difference" with other Indians with similar experiences.

"EK DEEWAR" (A WALL)

In some ways, the generation gap between Indian immigrants and their children is no different than the natural parent-child tensions experienced in other cultures. However, in most ways, this gap between Indian generations may be attributed to a difference in cultural orientation, rather than solely to generational differences.

Similarities do exist between some first and second generation Indians, primarily in what they are most and least interested in retaining about their Indian backgrounds. The samples from each generation showed that they were both committed to perpetuating Indian family values and religion, as well as many customs and traditions. On the other hand, individuals in both samples said they were least interested in retaining the caste system and division based on regional background in India; they also denigrated rituals, rigid food habits, and attitudes of inequality toward women (see Table IIIa). There was also some overlap between the two generations in terms of the circumstances under which they felt most or least "American" or integrated into American society (see Table IIIb). Over 90% of the immigrants said that they felt most a part of mainstream America with respect to their careers and professions, while

[9] L.A. Times, *5/25/90*

over 80% of the children said that they felt most integrated in terms of their educations. Similarly, when asked what aspects of American society made them feel least integrated, a majority of both first and second generation groups replied that their social attitudes and religious beliefs were not in tune with those of mainstream America. Said Haresh, 23, "American friends always ask me questions about why I still live at home, why we are always going to parties at other Indian friends' homes, why my parents don't like my dating so much. I guess our ways are hard for them to understand."

It is the differences between the generations, however, that account for much of the tension between parents and children. The differences lead one to believe that the second generation of Indians in America will set a political, social, and civic agenda of their own that will be quite different from that of their parents.

TABLE IIIa

WHAT MOST INTERESTED IN RETAINING ABOUT INDIAN CULTURE *

	Family Values	Religion	Traditions (Including Language)
1st gen	96%	75%	63%
2nd gen	92%	67%	58%

WHAT LEAST INTERESTED IN RETAINING ABOUT INDIAN CULTURE *

	Caste System/ Regional Division	Rigid Food Habits	Rituals	Attitude Toward Women
1st gen	46%	58%	52%	33%
2nd gen	67%	83%	63%	42%

* Note that some interviewees gave more than one response, so percentages total more than 100%.

TABLE IIIb

FIRST GENERATION CIRCUMSTANCES UNDER WHICH FEEL MOST "AMERICAN" *

Profession/Career	Social Attitudes/Behavior	Religion
92%	16%	0%

SECOND GENERATION CIRCUMSTANCES UNDER WHICH FEEL MOST "AMERICAN" *

Education	Social Attitudes/Behavior	Religion
83%	40%	0%

* Note that some interviewees gave more than one response, so percentages total more than 100%..

TIES TO INDIA:

As one would expect, the ties that children of immigrants feel to their homeland are not as strong as those felt by their parents. At the same time, it seems that the ties immigrants themselves feel toward India have not weakened to a notable extent. As mentioned earlier, many still visit India regularly and have family there. Said medical doctor Jitu, 45, "India is my motherland. I can never forget it." It is important to note that unlike many other immigrants, Indians can financially afford to visit their country. Also, visits to India are not hindered by political problems. The fact that immigrants are not forced to sever their ties with India may perpetuate the notion among both first and second generation Indians that they are not permanent citizens in the United States.

To second generation Indians, most of whom have never lived in India for an extended period of time, their "motherland" is what Indian writer V.S. Naipaul once referred to as an "area of darkness." Just as their parents relied on media images to form their opinions of the West, young Indian-Americans often rely on television and other news coverage to form their perceptions of India. Unfortunately, the Western media's portrayal of India is overwhelmingly negative. Said Raj, 21, "You look on TV, and all you see about India is people begging and starving in slums. Even if you are of Indian descent, you can't help but feel badly toward India after seeing this again and again." In addition to exposure to negative media images, many second generation Indians lack knowledge about their homeland and culture, simply because it is not part of their everyday existence. Bharati Mukherjee describes this aspect of young Indian-Americans in her works of fiction, "Babli wasn't tolerant of superstitions...If asked about Hinduism, all she'd ever said to her American friends was that 'it's neat'".[10]

Other children of immigrants who have actually visited India may also come away with mixed feelings. A majority of the interviewees said they felt that people in India treated them differently. Said Manoj, 19, "When I visited India, people used to either react to me like a celebrity because I was from 'the States,' or they would make fun of me because of my American accent. I never felt at home in India." Others felt disillusioned by the pervasive corruption and inefficiency in India. Said Aditya, 21, "There is bribery and cheating everywhere. People in power abuse it. The political problems are intense." He added, "When my parents go to India, they feel at peace, as if they have come home. I don't feel that way." This sense of alienation leads to a popular notion among the second generation that they are "neither here nor there," meaning that while in the United States, they do not feel completely American, and while in India, they do not feel genuinely Indian.

The positive feelings that second generation Indians had were more toward Indian culture and history, rather than toward the modern nation of India. Parents seem to understand the diminishing tie to India. Nevertheless, the thought that the bonds their descendants feel toward their country of origin are weakening is disconcerting for the immigrants. Similarly, the feeling of not "fitting in" in one's mother country is disturbing to their children.

ASSOCIATIONS:
As discussed in Chapter II, most immigrants associate socially almost exclusively with other Indians. Several, in fact, tend to

[10] *Mukherjee, p. 65*

associate predominantly with Indians from the same region in India. The groups most inclined to associate with individuals from the same region are Gujuratis, Punjabis, Sindhis, and certain South Indian communities, presumably due to a similarity in language and customs.

Among the second generation sampled, conversely, over 90% said that their friends were of mixed international backgrounds. The vast majority of those who had Indian friends, furthermore, said that an individual's regional ancestry in India played almost no part in their decision to associate with them. Said Ashish, 24, "Just because someone is a Guju *bhai* like me does not mean that I have to be friends with him."

There are several implications of the differences between parents and children on this particular issue. First, because second generation Indians have ventured into the world of associating with non-Indians even outside the school and work environment, they can be expected to assimilate into mainstream American society to a greater extent than their parents. Thus, their social attitudes as well as professional and political concerns will reflect their associations with non-Indians. Second, attitudes of regionalism and sectionalism perpetuated by immigrants have been a cause of disunity within the Indian community. These attitudes seem to be drastically reduced by the second generation, which will enable them to organize the Indian community in a way that their parents did not.

CAREER:

It is clear that, as a whole, Indian parents are ambitious for their children. Evidence shows that the second generation has responded well to parental emphasis on education and achievement. Indian-American students are regularly cited in publications as class valedictorians and winners of prestigious scholarships and awards. It is highly unusual, furthermore, for a second generation Indian not to seek a college education. The impetus to succeed academically seems related to the children's identification with the hardships parents faced as immigrants. Said Leela, 22, "My father worked very hard to establish himself here. It would all be a waste if his kids did not work hard and progress even further." The notion that in order to succeed one must be "one step ahead of everyone else" seems ingrained in the minds of immigrant children as well.

When asked about their ambitions for their children, more than half of the immigrants said that they would like them to be medical doctors. Their reasons included prestige, security, and a "good payoff." Others said that technical or scientific fields would be appropriate. The consensus seemed to be that Indians would not be as readily accepted in law, business, and other non-technical professions because not many Indians to date have made a mark in those fields.

Accordingly, the largest proportion of the second generation interviewees said they were presently pursuing medicine (see Table IIIc). A majority of those who were on the medical track said they initially chose the field primarily due to their parents' suggestion. The preponderance of young Indian "pre-meds," in fact, has become something of an institution in the Indian community.

TABLE IIIc

SECOND GENERATION SAMPLE FIELDS OF STUDY

	Medicine	Engineering & Related	Business	Other
Male	38%	25%	32%	5%
Female	30%	16%	25%	29%

Following the career path of one's parents' choosing is not uncommon. Said Jay, 24, "My parents forced me to be a computer scientist, and I couldn't really say no. They pushed me into it for the security, the money, and so they could brag about me to their friends." He continued, "The concept of interest not being a good enough reason to choose a career is very Indian. Americans do not understand this so well. My dad, himself, wanted to be a playwright, but his father forced him to take engineering because it was much more practical." This pattern is prevalent among the greater Asian American community as well. According to the 1980 IRCD Bulletin, Asian Americans are concentrated in fields where "technical knowledge rather than linguistic and social skills are at a premium." Labeled "occupational segregation," the career choice of Asian Americans "does not necessarily reflect aptitude, but rather an adaptive response to the world of reality as they have experienced it—a preoccupying concern for survival rather than consideration of aptitude, preference, and open choice".[11]

There are several implications of these patterns. First, as community activist Dr. Rajen Anand noted, "Few [Indian] parents let their children intellectually grow. They are intellectually stifled. They push their kids into medicine and engineering. If they are in business, they expect their children to do the same business." Added student leader Dhruv Gupta, "Indian parents want their kids to be financially secure above everything else. They are not encouraged to think for themselves." Still another student said, "It's okay to choose medicine or engineering, but you should do it because you like it, not because of the paycheck. Parents figure if you are making a lot of money, it doesn't matter if you are well-rounded intellectually or if you can develop an opinion of your own on all subjects."

The "pro-techie" attitude of Indian immigrants has hit home to a greater extent for some second generation Indians. One graduating senior, for instance, related how her parents would not finance a liberal arts private education for her because her brother wanted to attend a private medical school. "I understand that they [parents] can't afford two kids in a private school, but why is medicine worth the cash and English or history not worth it?"

The Indian community, then, can count on a future professional force similar, in some ways, to that of their parents. The level to which this generation will be satisfied pursuing occupations based primarily on material benefits remains to be seen. At the same time, relatively more Indian students, as well as more Asian-American students in general, are choosing non-

[11] *IRCD Bulletin, 1980*

Indian Immigrant Families

Indian-Americans make attempts to retain a sense of their culture even while living in the U.S.

The Indian Social Gathering

Second generation woman practicing classical Indian dance form of "Bharat Natyam"

Hindu shrine in immigrant's home

"Little Indias" are prominent in major American cities. Here, immigrant families can purchase food, ethnic costumes, or simply mingle with friends.

The many faces of second generation Indian-Americans

technical or non-scientific fields. The Indian English or history major is no longer as much of an anomaly as he or she was earlier. In a recent *Time* magazine article, an Asian comparative literature major noted that several young Asian-Americans are "more interested in public policy and social action than in what their parents preached about economic security through medicine and engineering".[12] Gradually, this trend will garner influence for Indian-Americans in other professional fields. Second generation Indians' foray into these professions will also test the popular belief that Indians are accepted and prosper in this country primarily due to their technical or scientific expertise.

What about the "underachieving children of overachieving parents?" In other words, how do Indian-Americans who do not live up to the "model minority" stereotype of being exceedingly conscientious students cope with the pressures to excel? When parents make blanket assumptions such as "all Indian kids are brilliant," how does the average or below-average student meet these expectations? The challenge that many young Indians face is that their parents pose a highly difficult act to follow. Said Shiv, 19, "When your dad makes it on his own in a foreign country as an internationally acclaimed research scientist, you have big shoes to fill." One parent, moreover, related that when her son did not gain admission into a private university and instead attended a state school, she considered this situation to be a major setback for the entire family. Some first generation as well as second generation Indians agreed that not all children of immigrants will have the same "hunger" or drive for success as their parents. Said Atul, 22, "When my dad first came here, he didn't have money to buy food. He used to go into restaurants and just eat ketchup. Not having anything is what motivated him to work. I haven't had the same hardships. My motivation to make it big is not as deep. Dad wanted it all. I want just enough."

Due to differing abilities, aptitudes, and interests, not all second generation Indians are destined to attend elite universities and choose professional careers. This fact lends further

[12] *Time, 3/25/91*

support to the notion that Indians will begin to enter fields other than those in which they currently prevail.

SOCIAL ISSUES:

> *I have been dating an American girl for four years. My parents don't know about it, and I don't want them to know. We sneak around and have had sex. Recently, my parents started looking for an Indian girl for me to marry. The main thing they look for is money. They don't understand my need to know and love a girl before I marry her. My mom and dad were introduced on a Monday and were married on that same Friday. I can't do that. No way.*
>
> —*Anonymous Indian male, 22*

The social behavior reflected in this statement represents the crux of the difference and source of greatest strife between the two generations. This situation induced writers Prakash N. Desai and George V. Coelho to conclude that "an Indian adolescent is perhaps the greatest source of anxiety to Indian immigrant parents." Two social issues are of central concern: dating and marriage. One may surmise that the second generation's uncertainty over these issues is, to a certain degree, a reflection of their confusion over broader identity issues.

As noted earlier, immigrants who came to this country in the mid- to late 1960s are not familiar with the concept of dating. In traditional families in India, it is still considered unconventional and improper for men and women to have pre-marital, romantic relationships. The problem, according to the second generation, is that parents do not understand what it means to date. Summarized one young woman, "Parents think dating means having sex. That is not the case with a lot of people." She went on to define dating as "basically a close friendship with the potential of evolving into something romantic or long-term." Despite parental restrictions, 95% of the sample of second generation said that they do date, but they were divided on the extent to which they inform their parents. Over half said that they preferred not to let their parents know if they were seeing anyone.

The parental reaction to the issue of dating was summarized by Neema, 47, mother of three, "Culturally, we are very different. It is very foreign for us to let our girls go out alone with boys. We never knew anything about dating and living together." Nevertheless, those parents who did let their children date admitted to maintaining separate standards for their sons and daughters. Said Dilip, 48, "It comes down to this: my daughter can get pregnant. My son can't."

Springing from concerns about dating are concerns about marriage. Among the parents interviewed, 90% said they preferred that their children choose Indian spouses. Indians are not unlike other minority or ethnic groups in their desire to keep marriage within the same group. The feeling is that Indian marriage partners would make the perpetuation of language, religion, and customs more likely. Parents feel that if their children married other Indians, it would be easier to incorporate them into their families. Said Pramod, 55, "If the girl my son marries is not Indian, she may not feel comfortable with our customs. Gradually, we would be less close to our son and to our future grandchildren. It would be easier for an Indian girl to become part of our family."

Interracial marriages, although still not the norm, are becoming less of a novelty, and many families have been able to compromise and accept the situation. A Hindu second generation woman, for instance, recently married a Mexican-American man. The couple participated in a traditional Hindu wedding in Indian attire. Shortly after the Hindu ceremony, they reappeared clad in a white bridal gown and a tuxedo to take Christian wedding vows, thereby appeasing both sides of the family. It seems that the main concern of first generation Indians is whether interracial marriages will last. Said one father of three, "Compatibility is important. A marriage has to have a backbone. Having Indian values in common is a strong foundation."

Many parents, however, remain rigid in their opposition to interracial relationships. Said Sridevi, 45, whose son is seriously involved with a Chinese-American woman, "Whatever he decides, he will have to live with it. If he believes he is madly in love, that is fine, but if she leaves him, he will have to deal with it. He has made his bed, now he must lie in it." Some families have suffered deep trauma as a result of dating and marriage-related tensions. At an Indian youth forum on dating and sexuality, one second generation woman broke down crying while explaining how her father disowned her as a result of her relationship with a white American man.

There is some agreement on the marriage issue between parents and children: sixty percent of parents said they are open to their children marrying Indian spouses of their own choosing, rather than opting for the traditional, arranged marriage. Said Laxmi, 49, "We can't keep our old standards of having our kids marry people from the same region and caste background. As long as the boy [my daughter chooses] is Indian, I don't really care what part of India he comes from."

Conflicts arise when the arranged marriage option is pushed on unwilling children. Approximately 75% of the second generation sampled said they preferred Indian spouses for the same reasons emphasized by their parents. However, 90% of those who want Indian spouses said they were averse to having an arranged marriage. Second generation Indians said that an arranged marriage connotes not spending an extended period of time getting to know the spouse-to-be and that the marriage is arranged according to the compatibility of the families, rather than that of the individuals. Said Neil, 20, "I don't buy the old line my parents give me: 'you love the person you marry, not marry the person you love.'" Several of those who preferred Indian spouses, however, said they would not mind being *introduced* to someone of their parents' choosing but wanted the freedom to get to know the person and take the relationship from that point.

A majority of the second generation interviewees who want to marry Indians said that it would be best for them to marry other "ABCD's" or Indians who grew up here, rather than have arranged marriages with partners directly from India. They said they wanted to share the commonality of their Indian-American backgrounds as well as avoid their partner's possible culture shock. Said Sangeeta, 22, "I don't want to deal with having to show my husband how to use an ATM or how to pump gas at a gas station."

More young men than women, however, said they may like to marry a woman raised in India and then bring her back to the States. Women seemed more averse to "importing" a spouse, primarily due to the Indian tradition of a woman moving to the man's home once they are married. A man following a woman to her home is perceived as dishonorable. Horror stories abound, furthermore, of foreign-born men marrying second generation women simply to obtain Green Cards. Some of these men have been known to leave or abuse their wives once they have attained their permanent resident status.

Modified ideas on social relations, then, will determine the very texture of the future Indian community. In other words, the incidence of interracial marriages will be linked to the extent to which "Indianness" is diluted in generations to come.

GENDER ROLES:

> *A person has to have sinned in his past life to be born a woman.*
>
> *—Ancient Indian proverb*

Among the more interesting aspects of this study proved to be the issue of gender roles and how they are perpetuated in the United States. None of the questions posed in the interviews were specifically related to this topic. Yet, the pattern of responses suggests that these issues were of concern to second generation Indian women, in particular.

Specific themes were illustrated by interviews with females of both generations. Among the first generation, several women said their immigration to the United States brought them independence and liberation from the institutional repression of women in India. Here they could run their households as they pleased and even hold jobs if they chose, free from the watchful eye and suffocation of the joint family arrangement, which normally includes a live-in mother-in-law. This new independence seems to have built self-esteem in the immigrant women. Said Rani, 40, "In India, a woman is evaluated on how she looks and sounds and on how well she can cook. If you are not very good-looking, you can be brought up with a lot of hang-ups." Added Neena, 41, "In India, a woman only has credibility as a wife and a mother. Here, you can be more than that."

While her mother feels increasingly liberated as an immigrant to the United States, the second generation Indian woman feels that old-world gender roles are still rigidly being upheld for her. Many young women asserted that a woman's worth in the eyes of the Indian community is not substantially increased by higher education. They said that the community consensus was that a bachelor's degree was necessary for a woman to have any "market value" as a suitable spouse, but graduate education led people to doubt how much time she could devote to being a wife and a mother. One young woman who was studying biology as an undergraduate was strongly discouraged by her parents to pursue medicine. She said, "My parents worried that if I spent so much time in med school, I would never have time to get married." She continued, "Throughout my life, society told me I could be whatever I wanted because I was smart and worked hard. Then, suddenly, I become of 'marriageable age,' and I'm told I have limits because I am a woman and should marry young. It makes me sick that women are still so defined by men."

These young women also feel oppressed by the traditional Indian image of an unmarried female that others impose upon them. For instance, the popular definition of a "good Indian girl" is one who does not date, is shy and delicate, and marries an Indian man of her parents' choosing. Career women are often perceived as too aggressive to be "feminine" or "tender." Said Sangeeta, 22, "How am I supposed to do well in this society and at the same time be delicate and fragile like a good little Indian woman?" She added that she overheard her parents say that it is not a good idea to educate and expose a young woman to a wide range of ideas, lest she become too "overqualified" to find a good husband.

Also of relevance is the second generation male's reaction to second generation women. As was discussed, most young Indian-Americans of both sexes who said they would like to marry Indians preferred to marry others like themselves—people of Indian ancestry, yet born and raised in this country. Surprisingly, however, several men who grew up in the United States had negative impressions of their female counterparts. Said Ashwin, 23, "I think all Indian girls who grew up here are psychologically messed-up. They either are too repressed by their parents, or they rebel and become total partiers and sleep around. I would never have anything to do with an Indian girl from America."

Furthermore, in an article entitled "Are Indian-American Men Sexist?", columnist Ankur Goel addressed concerns about Indian women who have grown up in the United States. He observed that in finding mates for their sons, parents often found Indian-American women "too free, too loose, and not homely enough." The better choice, according to these families, was "a woman from India, who could be expected to behave properly, because in India, service to husband and premarital chastity are still considered cherished virtues. The implication was that the women who have grown up here are unsuitable because they are too liberated".[13]

Second generation women reacted strongly to these generalizations. Said Deepa, 21, "So much is expected of us. We are supposed to excel in school and careers and still be demure and delicate, good mothers, wives, and daughter-in-laws. An Indian man can be a total buffoon but still expect to marry someone with all these qualities." Added another, "How can they [Indian-American men] think we won't have pre-marital relationships? A lot of American men find Indian women attractive. An Indian guy can date around, but if we do, we

[13] India West, *10/12/90*

become slutty." She continued, "I have a male Indian friend whom I know has had several intimate relationships with American women. He says, though, that he wants to marry an Indian and that she has to be a virgin."

This disillusionment of Indian-American women seemed corroborated by the fact that among the interviewees, more second generation men than women said they definitely wanted Indian spouses; specifically, *over half* of the Indian women sampled did not seem committed to marrying Indian men. The women reacted strongly to any implications that they had lost traditional values and were less "Indian" than women born and raised in India. Said Meera, 21, "Being Indian is what you feel in your heart. It is not whether you cook *sabji* and wear a *sari*. It is more related to your priorities, to the way you see the world. In that way, I think I and a lot of my [second generation female] friends are as Indian, if not more Indian, than girls in India."

None of the second generation men sampled expressed any insecurities about the possibility that second generation females may, in turn, react negatively to their attitudes. There is, however, an argument voiced frequently by Indian-American men that Indian women simply do not like Indian men, finding them sexist, physically unattractive, and "nerdy." These men add that white American women are not attracted to Indian men in the same way that white men are attracted to "exotic" Indian females. This situation is problematic to some young Indian-American men, although these feelings were not directly expressed by the interviewees.

Indeed, in an era in which women in their twenties are increasingly confident about their ability to be many things at once—wife, mother, professional—it is exceedingly frustrating for these women to be held to these antiquated standards within the confines of their own community. The level to which they conform to the standards imposed upon them remains to be seen. The current trend seems to be for these young women to pursue the careers of their choosing in the hope of finding

spouses, Indian or non-Indian, supportive of their needs for
fulfillment beyond the home.

A RAP SONG

On a lighter note, *India West* publisher Ramesh P. Murarka's
"Rap for Youth Awards Night" captures the essence of life as an
"ABCD:"

"Now here's a Rap, that's just for the youth,
    To get what they want, they'll fight nail & tooth.

Chorus: INDIAN YOUTH, INDIAN YOUTH...

Their roots go and ancestry, may go back to India,
    But their home, you see, is now in America.

They talk like Yanks, though their skin may be brown,
    On the accents of their parents, they often frown.

A problem in school, brings Mom in a hurry,
    But Mom, when you come, please don't wear a *sari*.

Hot dogs, hamburgers, fries and a shake,
    But Mom's *dal-roti*, I will not take.

It's O.K. for your parents, to want the best,
    But getting straight A's, is not the only test.

Don't worry so much, O' Mom & Dad,
    Have faith in us, we won't turn out so bad.

Music that you like, is by Shankar Jaikishan,
    But we'd rather hear, Janet Jackson.

We'll go to your parties, and wear a smile,
    But please before the next one, can we wait awhile.

Movies from India, we generally shun,
    Unless it's one, starring Amitabh Bachchan.

Our moms at parties, are demure and shy,
    But why take so long, to say good-bye.

Dad, oh Dad, may I please go out on a date?
    Yes, dear son, but don't be out too late.

Mom, dear Mom, may I please go out on a date?
    Sorry, dear daughter, but such is not your fate".[14]

[14]India West, 7/6/90

Bridging the Gap: A Solution

AWARENESS AND COMMUNICATION:

A major finding of this study is that although some parents are attuned to the problems of growing up between two cultures, most lack genuine awareness and adequate means of helping children through the problems they are facing. Second generation Indians seem to feel that their parents' attention is focused primarily on the children's economic future, rather than their overall psychological development. Inadequate communication in many Indian households is the cause of severe tensions.

There is a plausible explanation for this apparent lack of awareness and communication. Indian immigrant parents stress the importance of financial security and economic well-being to their children because it has been a prevalent issue in their own lives. In India, support of one's extended family and the sense of healthy psychological development that it instills are taken as "givens." It is economic success, especially for the middle class, that is uncertain. While in the United States, especially post-1980s United States, it is the exact reverse. If one is educated and determined, one can achieve a certain amount of financial success. Healthy relationships, both with family and friends, and other aspects of a support structure are not assumed and need to be cultivated and constantly reaffirmed. Thus, Indian parents and children seem to have different orientations regarding goals to work toward in life. There is a profound difference in their social grounding. Without communication, it would be difficult for each group to understand the other's motivations and actions.

Evidence suggests that parental awareness of the types of pressures and strains faced by children is minimal. An Indian-American publication, for instance, featured an article on the second generation, calling them "God's blessed children." The author elaborated:

They have the best of all worlds, say many parents, whose path to prosperity has been far more sinuous and tortuous than their children probably ever encounter. Large homes in suburbia, a car to a child, tennis courts, music lessons, clothes from Saks Fifth and Marshall Fields, skiing vacations and holidays abroad. The knowledge that parents can pay Ivy League tuition fee, all they have to do is get the grades.[15]

This passage reflects the popular misconception among immigrant parents that if a child has material comforts and economic security, he or she is "set for life." Their children, on the other hand, assert that their lives are fraught with difficult dilemmas that often leave them feeling alienated and confused. These children feel that their parents are not highly sensitive to these dilemmas. Said Arjun, 18, "You go to school and all around you are these temptations to do things that are supposed to be against your Indian culture. You may not give in to the temptations, but they are there. Sometimes, it can make you crazy." Added Kiran, 19, "Your [American] friends think there's something wrong with you because you don't date and chase after boys. You don't do it because it would make your parents mad. Every single day is a balancing act. You constantly have to explain yourself—either to your parents or to your American friends."

The significance of this situation lies in the fact that *over 90%* of the second generation interviewed said that their parents were extremely unaware of the pressures and dilemmas they face outside the home. For instance, those who had relationships with the opposite sex said their parents do not realize what it entails. Said one college student, "If parents know [that a person is dating someone], they assume it is a hand-holding relationship." Another student asserted that he thought 50-75% of Indian-American college-age students are sexually active and that 40-50% had experimented with drugs. "Parents have no clue," he said. "The classic attitude is 'not my kid.'" Said one second generation woman who aborted her child due to a

[15] India Abroad, *10/13/89*

pregnancy out of wedlock, "If my parents had seemed even the slightest bit open to listening to me, I might not have gotten myself into this mess."

Many immigrants did, however, concede that their offspring's childhood is much less "carefree" than their own in India. Said Neema, 44, "Our children certainly have more in the way of material things and opportunities for the future, but life here makes you grow up fast. When we were younger, you never worried as long as your parents were there. In fact, you were never really considered responsible for yourself as long as your parents were alive."

Linked with minimal parental awareness is the lack of communication between parents and children, according to the second generation Indians interviewed. In the September 1990 Convention of National Federation of Indian-American Associations held in San Jose, California, communication was repeatedly stressed in various family workshops as a key to avoiding family tension, especially tension between parents and adolescent children. In his opening remarks, Dr. Jagat Motwani observed, "We [Indian parents] don't encourage children to talk. We mistake communication for disrespect." Youth shared experiences where they felt better communication with their parents would have solved certain problems. Said one student, "When I asked to go to the high school prom, my parents said, 'No, *beta* [child]. Indian children don't do these things.' They wouldn't give me their permission, so I went without telling them. I didn't want to sneak around, but what could I do?" A parent, in turn, suggested that the child could help the situation by initiating communication, perhaps by explaining what a high school prom is and its significance as an American rite of passage.

In some cases, the consequences of a lack of awareness or ineffective communication have been severe. Some young Indians have been driven to extreme behavior such as substance abuse and sexual promiscuity. As far as a solution is concerned, the second generation desires a greater level of sensitivity from their parents as to the trials of growing up both Indian and

American. Awareness and sensitivity, they asserted, would render their parents more helpful in the process of reconciling dual identities. Both generations concurred that awareness and sensitivity can primarily be achieved primarily through communication, and this communication can be initiated by either party—parent or child.

TEACHING CULTURE:

> *I don't want my house to be walled-in on all sides and my windows to be blinded. I want the cultures of all lands to blow about my house freely. But I refuse to be blown off my feet by any.*
> —*Mahatma Gandhi*

A second solution for lessening the parent-child gap evident from the interview data relates to the teaching of culture. To many, "culture" is an amorphous term. Even so, it seems that many immigrants have a unilateral definition of culture. To them, culture is represented by vestiges of their distant homeland: language, food, religion, art, music, dance, customs, rituals, and traditions. Immigrant parents frantically attempt to pass these aspects of culture on to their children. The objective is to shelter their offspring from things "American," which is roughly defined as anything not "Indian." Their anxiety is exacerbated by the fact that they have the sole responsibility of teaching culture; while in India, one's extended family of grandparents, aunts, uncles, and cousins helps to instill identity and tradition in children.

Over half of the second generation individuals interviewed argued that many immigrants lack a clear understanding of American culture. The second generation felt that their parents unfairly label American culture as inferior to Indian culture. Pradeep, 18, explained that his parents often cite a high divorce rate, drug and alcohol abuse, and overall breakdown of the family structure as reasons to resist adopting American culture. Pradeep felt, however, that American *professional* families had goals similar to those of Indian families—namely, safe and secure futures for their children. He felt that an increased effort to get to know white American people would prevent first generation Indians from forming negative stereotypes. Veera, 42, an immigrant with several white American friends, agreed, "Professional families in America share the same values. However, Indian immigrants confuse the values of lower socio-economic groups in America with those of the American population as a whole."

The second generation felt that the "cultural fence" their parents build around them is not working to the children's advantage. Growing up with the notion that they are not supposed to adopt aspects of American culture is causing confusion in the minds of young Indian-Americans. It is clear, though, that they are asking for their elders' assistance in forging an identity. As explained earlier, the process of coming to terms with identity starts at a young age, not necessarily at adolescence. One college student, for instance, related that when she was six years old, her mother came to pick her up from school dressed in the traditional Indian *sari* and *bindi*. Her friends asked her why her mother was wearing a bedsheet and had a thumbtack through her forehead. She said that at that young age, she started to form some very definite ideas about what it means to be Indian. She added, "I'm not saying Indian moms should wear polyester pantsuits instead of their traditional clothes. All I'm saying is that if you're going to do things like that, you need to prepare your kids for it."

What second generation children want is to be taught a "*dual culture.*" They need to be given the sense that they are both Indian *and* American, not Indian guests in a foreign land. Children want to communicate to their parents that being "Americanized" does not necessarily mean absorbing the negatives of Western culture; it relates to integrating the positives of American culture into the already rich cultural heritage of India. The interviewees, for instance, described the "ideal" qualities for both Indian and American youth. The young Indian is determined, studious, focused, and family-oriented, while the young American is self-confident, independent, and well-rounded. Establishing a sense of both Indian and American is the goal toward which second generation Indians want to strive.

This synthesis, at once, represents both a challenge and an opportunity for immigrant parents. As Dr. Arunadhati Perkash wrote in her "Raising Children in Two Cultures," Indian parents have a chance "to prune out the outmoded, preserve the relevant, and nurture the most positive aspects of the Indian cultural heritage for their children." The second generation wants to move away from the indoctrination, "force-feeding," and symbolic gestures of culture that the immigrant population tries to impose on them. For example, as an opinion letter on raising children in the U.S. recently stated, "Learning *Bharata Natyam* in my opinion does not mean you are learning Indian culture. All it means is that you are learning a dance form that originated in India. After all, learning ballet does not make you Russian!".[16] Perhaps the parents' ability to assist in the process of reconciling dual identity is a function of the immigrants' defining their own place in American society.

[16] India Abroad, *3/15/91*

Okasan/Mother

twenty five years she's been here
and still
    a-me-ri-ka makes her mouth sour tight
    sticks in her mind like spit-wet thread
    caught in the eye of a needle.
twenty-five years
and still
    she tells no stories of war to a daughter
    she saves marriage lace and
    satin baby kimonos in a cedar chest for
    a daughter who denies her conversation
twenty-five years of city living
people calling her oriental or chinese
sometimes jap
and still
    her eyes, like teardrops turned sideways,
    say nothing.
    with pride, she writes from right to left
    of the greatness of a-me-ri-ka to her people.
twenty-five years
alone.
still
she cries in japanese

                —Sakae S. Roberson
     (in Making Waves: An Anthology of Writings By
          and About Asian American Women)

CHAPTER IV

———————————•◆•———————————

FINDING A PLACE IN AMERICA

A HYPOTHESIS

As addressed earlier, the post-1965 Indian immigrant's experience has been different from that of other immigrant groups in many respects. Several factors have provided for a relatively smooth transition into economic well-being. Indian immigrants had the calling cards of English proficiency and high levels of education. The fact that they are geographically dispersed, meaning that there are no "Indian ghettos," shelters them to a large extent from discrimination against the ethnic group as a whole. One may also argue that the current generation of American adults, many of whom were a product of the 1960s, have a romantic perception of India, rendering them more accepting to immigrants from that land. Yet, as decades pass, one sees these immigrants facing certain challenges—specifically, questions regarding their place in the United States. The way in which the immigrant generation chooses to recognize and respond to these challenges will directly affect their children's generation. It becomes relevant, then, to address the nature of "assimilation" of these immigrants.

CULTURAL COPING OVER TIME

It is clear that as professional success is achieved, the Indian immigrant community faces other tensions. Changing family values and increasingly stark differences between the first and second generations are among these concerns. Nevertheless, it seems that the immigrant population is facing challenges related to their *own* convictions, values, and futures. The most unnerving and urgent of these questions is, 'After we have achieved professional success, what next?' Robin Podder, who wrote and produced a play on the dilemmas faced by Indian immigrants in the U.S., described the situation, "Indians in this country are torn on the question of what is success. These people came here from modest economic backgrounds and were bewildered by the amount of money they could make. Once they make the money, they wonder what to do next."

Said Gautam, 46, "I never tell my wife or kids, but I wonder if we made the right decision to come here. We have all the possessions we could ever want, but what about culture and values and family? What have we given up to have all these *things*?" After accomplishing all that they set out to do, then, Indian immigrants seem to question the meaning of their lives in the United States.

This sense of confusion after achieving economic sucess may be considered a classic American dilemma. One may argue that in American culture, "making it big" financially is a primary goal to many people. Once that goal is attained, it is archetypical of the American experience to say, "What next?" It might be argued that immigrants pursue the American Dream more intensely than even the average American because the immigrants have more at stake—they have left their country and, in most cases, have no one to rely upon but themselves. Consequently, these immigrants experience the dilemmas and doubts that accompany the attainment of the American Dream more intensely as well.

In a different way, the immigrant experiences a "neither here nor there" sentiment of his own. Indian writer J. Rajgopal labels this predicament the "$X + 1$" Syndrome. The theory is that the early years of the immigrant's experience are spent in pursuit of the American Dream. Once that is attained, thoughts of returning to India occur to the immigrant:

> With all the material comforts that money can bring, begins the first signs of uneasiness—a feeling that somehow things are not what they should be. The craze for exotic electronic goods, cars and vacations has been satiated. The weekend gatherings are becoming routine. Faced with a mid-life crisis, the upwardly mobile Indian's career graph plateaus out. Younger and more aggressive Americans are promoted. At the home front, the children have grown up and along with American accents have imbibed American habits (cartoons, hamburgers) and values (dating). They respond to their parents' exhortation of leading a clean Indian way of life by asking endless questions. The generation gap combines with the cultural chasm. Not surprisingly, the first serious thoughts of returning to India occur at this stage.

The immigrants find, though, that leaving the States has definite complications. Their children feel that this is their home. Moreover, after having spent more years abroad than in India, immigrant themselves feel out of their element in their mother country. Inefficiency, bureaucracy, corruption, and a lack of opportunities still render India an impractical option. The decision to return to India is thus indefinitely postponed:

> In other words if X is the current year, then the objective is to return in the $X + 1$ year. Since X is a changing variable, the objective is never reached. Unable to truly melt into the "Great Melting Pot," chained to his cultural moorings and haunted by an abject fear of giving up an accustomed standard of

living, the Non Resident Indian vacillates and oscillates between two worlds in a twilight zone.

In his article entitled "The Indo-American Lives a Marginal Existence," journalist Francis Assisi argues that the heart of the dilemma is that the average Indian immigrant is never truly able to balance the Indian and American aspects of his life—he lives on the margin. Furthermore, it is difficult for the immigrant to foster "the best of both worlds" idea in his children because he has not achieved this balance himself. Assisi explains that the Indian immigrant "becomes essentially a homeless man, missing India when he is in America; missing America when he is in India. The tragedy of his predicament is that even if he were to succeed in integrating the two life-styles, he would still remain a homeless man, a marginal man, in that neither society can fulfill all the strivings and urges of his being. He thus becomes a caricature of his true persona; a misfit par excellence".[1] As a solution, Assisi suggests that the immigrant face the consequences of his migration and recognize and accept his marginal existence. Perhaps the mental anguish of the marginal immigrant would be alleviated if he made concrete attempts to define his place in American society.

CULTURAL PLURALISM

The present intellectual climate in the United States is conducive to the Indian immigrants' efforts to find their place in American society. Multiculturalism is the buzzword of the decade. *Time* magazine states that we are currently witnessing the "browning of America." Historian Arthur Schlesinger, Jr., furthermore, articulates the trend toward modifying the traditional notion of the "melting pot." He notes, "The contemporary ideal is not assimilation but ethnicity. We used to say *e pluribus unum*. Now we glorify *pluribus* and belittle *unum*." [2]

It is fortunate that the melting pot is currently being repudiated in American society, for it is an especially unsuitable paradigm to apply to the Indian community—one that is so committed, both in the first generation and in a substantial

[1] Indo-Americans: A Historical Perspective, *p. 7*
[2] L.A. Times, *1/13/91*

proportion of second generation, to preserving its culture. Given their priorities, it seems that the model most applicable to the Indian community is cultural pluralism. This model affirms both the maintenance of separate ethnic identities and full participation in the professional, social, and political activities of American society; it does not dictate an abandonment of ethnic identity for the sake of becoming an indistinguishable part of the melting pot. Cultural pluralism thus suggests more of a "salad bowl" approach. In *The Asian Indian Experience in the United States*, sociologist Parmatma Saran argues:

> The Asian Indians in America not only show a clear preference for the cultural pluralism model, but also see it as the most desirable and acceptable from their point of view, as well as its being in the larger interests of American society...In contrast to older immigrant groups, Indians, as well as other new ethnic groups, have the advantage of less pressure for Americanization.[3]

THE JEWISH MODEL

Although there are many differences between the Jewish-American and Indian-American communities, there are enough similarities between the groups to justify using Jews as a model for preserving culture while still participating in mainstream American life. One may deduce that a characteristic of Jewish-Americans is their commitment to maintaining their culture. Jews in America oppose the phenomenon of "upwardly mobile individuals" losing a sense of their ethnic identity; the Jewish community has been able to deal with a "shift in social class," while still retaining its ethnic "integrity".[4]

Raymond Wolfinger's views on the three levels of "absorption of immigrants into American society" helps to define the differences between the melting pot and multicultural approaches. He identifies the first level of absorption as "acculturation," which refers to adopting the structural aspects of the dominant society, including conversing in English, obtaining

[3] *Saran, p. 11, 116*
[4] *De Vos, p. 25*

higher levels of education and income, and involvement in the economic, social, and cultural aspects of society. The second level is "association," where groups begin to behave like non-ethnics in terms of a general lack of separatism from mainstream society. The third level is "assimilation," which refers to the "disappearance of ethnicity as a source of identity".[5] Jewish-Americans, according to Wolfinger, "have attained a high degree of acculturation in that their income, educational, and occupational levels are higher than average. They are much less 'associated,' and their ethnic consciousness is high".[6] Similarly, despite a high potential for "acculturation" given their proficiency in English, Indians have thus far remained very much in tune with the traditions and customs of their Indian upbringing.

MOVING AWAY FROM "NEITHER HERE NOR THERE"

Since the cultural pluralism model provides a way for Indians in the United States to maintain their culture and participate in the varied aspects of American society, perhaps the Indian community should make a concerted effort to do just that. Trends evident from interviews as well as from conferences and publications indicate that the time is right for the community to make a commitment to the United States as their *permanent home* and, consequently, to participate to a greater extent. Said Rahul, 53, "Immigrants lack convictions. We need to make some decisions. We need to ask ourselves, 'Do we want to live in this country?' If we do, we have to feel this is our country and get involved." As Chandu Radia, columnist for I*ndia Abroad,* explains:

> People will not judge our culture merely on the basis of the *Bharata Natyam* and *Raas Garba* performances or the various rituals at festivals. Nor will our success and contributions be measured merely by the price tags of our cars, sizes of our homes or academic performances of our children.

[5] *Wolfinger, p. 32*
[6] *Wolfinger, p. 32*

Our culture (and, to a large degree, our success) will mostly be judged by our behavior and attitudes in every day life and how well we fulfill our responsibilities of participating in and contributing to local cultural activities.[7]

It seems that the process of making a stronger commitment to the United States as their permanent home will empower the immigrants to foster a more practical and positive sense of identity in their children—one that does not revolve around the concept of holding oneself aloof from an alien society. By undergoing this process, both generations will be able to move away from "neither here nor there" sentiments toward "both here and there" ways of thinking.

[7] India Abroad, *4/5/91*

Man is a political animal.
—Aristotle

A community is like a ship; everyone
ought to be prepared to take the helm
—Henrik Ibsen

CHAPTER V

PARTICIPATION IN
AMERICAN SOCIETY

A MANDATE FOR PARTICIPATION

One would be hard pressed to say that Indian immigrants have
not assimilated in a broad sense of the word. For reasons
already discussed, their level of "structural assimilation,"
meaning participation in the institutional spheres of work and
education, is high. Nevertheless, a major conclusion of this
study is that greater political, social, and civic involvement in
American society is essential for the Indian community's future
success. Participation may not only be a means for the community to accept the United States as its permanent home, but it
may also be the most important element the immigrants pass
on to their children.

The clear consensus among the second generation sampled
was that a legacy of involvement is what they most require from

their parents at this junction in their lives. Young Indian-Americans feel that trying to maintian an existence separate from the mainstream American population not only adversely affects the second generation's efforts to develop their own identities, but may also make them open to discrimination and prejudice in the future. As addressed in Chapter III, the children of Indian parents are still perceived as different from the "norm," due to name, skin color, and a variety of other reasons, despite the fact that they were born and raised in the United States.

Furthermore, as many second generation Indians may not choose professional careers, they may not have the "power of the dollar" that the first generation currently has. For instance, Indian-American political leaders believe that if Indians in America have one political "trump card," it is that they are among the most affluent of all ethnic communities in the country. Without economic muscle, however, the second generation may be more susceptible to a negative backlash, if they do not gain influence in other areas. Said one Indian-American who is planning a career in public service, "Acquiring a reputation for giving back to the country from which we have gained so much is to our [community's] advantage. It might help us avoid the bad experiences Indians have had in places like Fiji, Uganda, and England." In general, second generation Indians feel that a commitment to participate from their parents would carry the same importance in the long run as their efforts to provide education, financial security, and a sense of Indian culture for their children.

REASONS FOR LIMITED INVOLVEMENT

Although recent progress has been made in the political realm, the interviewees themselves observed that Indians do not participate to a notable extent in American social, civic, and political activities. Numerous factors account for this lack of participation. Many immigrants interviewed asserted that to them, survival and economic security were still of the highest priority. Said Baldev, 49, "As an immigrant, you are always insecure, no matter how much you have. You feel like if you don't concentrate on your work, it can all get taken away from you."

Another important factor is the traditional Indian distaste for politics and volunteerism. One interviewee explained that in India, political participation is left to go*ondas* or hoodlums and is perceived as a game fraught with corruption and dishonesty. Indians in America, moreover, seem to keep up with political events but view direct participation as exclusively reserved for "WASPs" or "old money." A popular saying captures Indian attitudes toward political participation in both countries: "In America, you get rich and then go into politics. In India, you go into politics and then get rich." In terms of the outlook toward volunteerism, the average Indian feels a strong sense of responsibility toward his family, but not necessarily toward his community. In a speech to a gathering of Indian professionals, former Indian Ambassor to the United States K.S. Bajpai explained, "Indian philosophy emphasizes man in relation to God, man in relation to nature, and man in relation to the hereafter. But man in relation to man has not been one of our strong points."

The immigrant attitude toward the United States is also of relevance. The X + *1* Syndrome and theories of marginal existence discussed in Chapter IV support the argument that perhaps many immigrants have not accepted the U.S. as their permanent home. The desire to participate in this country's affairs, then, remains minimal. It is not unusual to see immigrants becoming more involved and emotional about Indian political and social issues than they are about American issues. Many first generation Indians interviewed also pointed out that because they did not come to this nation as refugees but, rather, because their skills were desired and solicited by American society, the impetus to give back to the nation is not as great.

Internally, moreover, the Indian community is not united. Regional background in India often determines the people with whom one will associate. Several Indian political leaders said that immigrants have refused to support certain causes or events because the organizers of the group were of a different regional background. Political activist Rajen Anand noted that there are eight to ten Gujurati associations alone in southern California and over sixty associations for people of Indian origin in the greater Los Angeles area, most of which are organized according to regional categories. "Hopefully, we can start to think of ourselves as Indian, rather than Gujurati or Punjabi or whatever," said Anand. The fact that there are few areas in which Indians are geographically concentrated works both to the community's advantage and disadvantage. In other words, their geographic dispersal may generate a low profile and protect them from prejudice and resentment, but it also deprives them of the strength in numbers needed at election time.

THE INDIAN-AMERICAN POLITICAL SCENE

The Indian community has made some genuine and, to a certain degree, successful efforts to become politically involved. Some Indian-Americans have received appointments to prestigious government posts. As indicated by the tone of many forums and gatherings, an increased sense of the need to get politically involved is prevalent within the professional Indian community. Said Inder Singh, president of the National Federation of Indian-American Associations, "Our concerns started with education, then career, then marriage and family, then social recognition and now, finally, we are concentrating on political participation. It is like a ladder. We have taken it one step at a time." The fact that cultural organizations are losing ground to political groups such as the Indo-American Political Association (IAPA), the Indian-American Political Action Committee (IAPAC), and the Indian-American Foundation for Political Education (IAFPE) illustrates increasing interest. Several community leaders maintain that it is the affluent, professional Indians who have the resources to lead the effort to gain political influence.

Certain observations can be made regarding the current Indian political effort. First, it is essential to consider the characteristics of the typical politically-involved Indian: in general, this person is a man, over 40, highly affluent, and established in a professional career. Political functions usually entail inviting a senator or congressman to one of the community member's homes or to a restaurant for an evening of Indian cuisine, with guests paying anywhere from $50 to $100 per head to attend. According to Anand, the typical Indian politico is interested in glamor and publicity and not necessarily in supporting any particular cause; to some, this kind of involvement is simply "photo opportunity politics."

In the course of research, I attended a number of political functions. One of these events was a fundraising lunch in the Los Angeles area for two out-of-state congressmen. This particular event was highly typical of most Indian political gatherings. The congressmen were several hours late and said very little of relevance to India or to Indians in the U.S. While they were speaking, several guests continued to talk among themselves. During the question-answer period, over twenty members of the executive committee of the political association sponsoring the lunch spoke on the same issues. The executives of the association had apparently drafted a resolution regarding civil strife in the Indian state of Kashmir and wanted the congressmen to respond to it. The second primary issue was American policy regarding the licensing of foreign medical graduates. There were few women present; those who were there did not speak or interact with the congressmen. Also, there were no second generation Indians present or even invited, according to one of the association's officers.

This scenario lends support to the criticisms of the way in which Indians presently go about seeking political clout. Many people asserted that these organizations were not at all open to outsiders. Said one immigrant, "Only rich doctors and businessmen can go to these things. Even if someone else were to go, the organizers hog all the limelight. They already have preset agendas, so you don't even get a chance to speak." In addition, the fact that few women or second generation Indians generally participate leads one to question the types of issues supported by a group of middle-aged, affluent men. In other words, do current political efforts reflect the concerns of the Indian community as a whole?

THE SECOND GENERATION AND POLITICAL INVOLVEMENT

Comparing first and second generation responses with respect to political interest and awareness shows that the children of immigrants have a much higher degree of interest in participating in the American political system than their parents. There was little difference between both generations in terms of their level of political awareness—a majority of both samples said they kept up with American current events through the newspaper and television. When asked about direct involvement, however, 70% of the first generation sample said that they felt there was no way to be involved other than by contributing funds. Commented Bhushan, 49, "We immigrants definitely feel an element of detachment, like we can't influence things." Among those second generation individuals sampled, on the other hand, 80% said they felt there were other ways to be involved in the political sphere besides contributing money. Only 4% of the second generation interviewees, however, said they would consider careers in public service or government.

A big issue for the second generation is the alienation they feel from first generation political organizations. These associations, it seems, form superficial "youth wings," with the intention of involving young people in their efforts. Nevertheless, these wings usually dissolve within a few months, and little opportunity is given to young people to be involved in a meaningful way. They are rarely included, for instance, at the fundraising functions. Said government major Nakul, 21, "Our parents run around saying how they form these groups to help us [the second generation], but they never give us a chance to get involved. I think it's more because some of these men like the sound of their own voices." Community leader and attorney Hari Lal said he observed a "fundamental clash in the political thoughts of immigrants and the second generation." He continued, "It is going to be tremendously difficult for young people to come in unless they are strong and aggressive. The older generation will not make leeway for them."

Some young Indian-Americans who have attempted to get involved in the youth wings said they were very turned-off by the pettiness that can prevail in these organizations. Said one college student, "The ego thing for these people sometimes gets outrageous. Also, they are so hung up on who is a Gujurati and who is a Madrasi that they don't get anything done. It splits the community up, rather than bringing it together."

Others said they felt that the first generation did not recognize that many young people have reached college age and, in some cases, know a great deal more about the American political system than the first generation. These young people felt it would be advantageous to the Indian community as a whole to incorporate more people of the second generation into these organizations. A first generation interviewee, however, explained that Indian immigrants do not have a specific political agenda. He said, "Our goals are different from [those of] the kids. The second generation needs to stop criticizing mom and dad, get off their behinds, and stand up and speak out."

In any event, it is clear that the political agenda of the second generation will be quite different from that of their parents' generation. Those who are politically interested argued that issues relating to Indo-U.S. relations and Indian domestic issues are definitely important because the way in which India as a nation is perceived affects the way Indians abroad are perceived. The second generation's emphasis, however, will be on minority and civil rights issues or issues that concern Indians in the United States. Said attorney and political activist Ankur Goel, himself a second generation Indian, "Most of us will not be as concerned with India as our parents. We will not have the same kind of unanimity on those issues. On the Kashmir issue, for instance, more of us will be willing to fault India. We are less concerned with territorialism."

The approach the second generation follows is also likely to be different. Its spokesmen contend that political involvement will not be as personality and ego-related as it is for the first generation. Said Goel, "For us, getting our picture in *India West* with a congressman is not the number-one goal. We will want to be leaders in general, not just leaders of the Indian community It won't be the end-all goal for us to be powerful within the Indian community." The second generation political agenda will be more cause or issue-oriented, and efforts will be made to form coalitions with other minority or ethnic groups with the same objectives.

Many concur that the children of immigrants will form their own organizations to meet their needs. This effort has already been initiated by what some call the "one-and-a-half generation," comprised of Indian-Americans in their early- to mid-thirties, who have spent most of their lives outside of India. Their methods are more at the grassroots level, which attracts people from a wider age and economic spectrum. Bay Area-based attorney Mohinder Mann has spearheaded such an organization in northern California. He said, "The younger generation is turned off by the older generation's fighting among themselves. If they don't incorporate young people, they may lose their kids to a vacuum." To combat this outcome, Mann's organization tries to incorporate the "common Indian-American" into the political process by inviting diverse groups to casual soirees with local political figures at people's homes. "We are trying to avoid separating ourselves from the masses of the Indian community, as other big organizations currently do. We do not want four or five elite people controlling the whole thing from the top."

SOLUTIONS

It is evident that including and working with the second generation of Indians would be a positive step toward acquiring political influence. The second generation will succeed where many immigrants have failed—namely, in interaction and communication with mainstream American people. The impact of the Indian community can be made stronger if they would attempt to lessen internal divisions based on regional background as well as integrate their children's generation into their activities. Coalition-building with other minority communities, especially Asian groups, will also be conducive to the Indian political purpose. Many observers argue that Indians should also attempt to support candidates from within their own community, rather than simply funding white American candidates.

It is not truly just to pass judgment on the Indian community's level of political interest, thus far. In the approximately twenty-five years that they have been here they have achieved far more than most other immigrant and native communities. Their level of apathy, in fact, may simply reflect the general American population's attitude toward government and politics. It is important for Indians in the U.S. to note that their participation in American society is not limited solely to national political involvement. Participation in local politics and civic affairs is also appropriate.

The most significant result of an effort to get involved in the various spheres of American life may be the impact it has on the second generation. In addition to providing the political influence to protect the community from a future discriminatory backlash, involvement would instill a sense of belonging in children of Indian origin born and raised in the United States.

Hema, 44, nevertheless, articulated the emotional and psychological difficulties the immigrant faces in attempting to be involved in mainstream America: "To foreigners, 'American society' is an unknown quantity. I have seen Indians struggle so hard to be involved in a meaningful way. The Indian immigrant is bright. He [or she] is not simply a passive or reactive being. It is not that they [the immigrants] cannot work in tandem with the younger generation. The maturity of the youngsters will show when they demonstrate some sensitivity to the immigrants' insecurities and the difficulties they have faced in the past."

Indian-Americans concede that there is still much progress to be made. Yet, the words of Goethe seem to illuminate a course of action, "Whatever you can do or dream you can do, begin..."

The stranger that soujourneth with you shall be unto you as the home-born among you.

—Leviticus 15:34

CHAPTER VI

CONCLUSION

RECAP

A number of significant findings and recommendations for the Indian-American community emerged in the course of this study:

- Indians who immigrated as a result of the 1965 Immigration Act are different from early and contemporary immigrant groups in many ways, primarily in their high level of education and concentration in the science and technical professional fields. This background propelled them into the higher socio-economic levels of American society in a short period of time.

- The adaptation of the second generation is of specific importance to both generations. These children of immigrants have faced and continue to face the challenge of balancing two very different cultures. This questioning of identity begins at a young age and continues for an indefinite period; in other words, it is not simply a phase of adolescence.

- The concerns of second generation Indians differ from those of other second generation Asians in several ways—most notably, Indians view pre-marital male-female dating and courtship as improper and unconventional. Also, a majority of Indian immigrants are either Hindu, Muslim, or Sikh, preventing them from assimilating into American society on a religious level, as many Asians have been able to do.

- In college, a majority of second generation Indians come to terms with their Indian background and start to view it more positively.

- There are stark differences between the first and second generations with respect to their ties to India, social associations, career choices, attitudes toward issues such as dating and marriage, and ideas about gender roles.

- A possible means to bridging the generational and cultural gap is greater parental *awareness* regarding dilemmas faced by children as well as greater *communication.*

- Sensitivity to one another's concerns is inherently challenging because of the different orientations of each group: parents' main concern is economic well-being, while children are also seeking to cultivate and maintain a positive social support system.

- Immigrants at this juncture are facing a dilemma of their own, doubting their future happiness in this country. Yet, returning to India permanently is not an attractive option for the immigrants, due to possible difficulties readapting to India coupled with the fact that the vast majority of the children of immigrants will continue to live in the United States.

- Reconciling the immigrant's place in America is a means of alleviating their dilemma. In this sense, cultural pluralism is a viable method for immigrants to retain their culture and participate in American society.

Given the responses from both the first and second generation interviewees, it seems that the following is needed for the community at this juncture:

- Children of immigrants need to be taught that they are both Indian and American, not foreigners in the United States; the second generation seeks a philosophy of *dual culture*.

- To facilitate this dual culture mode of thought, immigrants should rethink their perceptions of American culture as well as their definition of culture in general. Immigrants should ask themselves what positive aspects of American culture can be incorporated into what they teach their children.

- A commitment to participate in the political, civic, and social realms of American society is needed, not only to protect the community from future negative reactions but also to instill dual culture and a heightened sense of belonging in their children.

- At the same time, the second generation should be sensitive to the limitations of their parents' generation and take as much initiative as possible in developing their own definitions of culture and identity, as well as in creating their own political and social agenda.

AMERICA IS HOME

It is clear that there will continue to be a significant population of Indians in the United States. The first generation was divided on the question of whether they would make the choice to immigrate again, knowing what they know now. Sixty percent said that they would immigrate, and 40% said they would not (see Table VI a). One interviewee who said he would not immigrate again argued, "In India, you don't have a frenetic search for happiness. Life just happens to you." *One hundred percent* of the second generation interviewed, nonetheless, said that if they could have influenced their parents' choice to immigrate, they would definitely have urged them to come to this country. All of those interviewed also planned on remaining permanently in the United States.

TABLE VIa

WOULD YOU IMMIGRATE AGAIN?

	Yes	No
Male	33%	17%
Female	27%	23%
TOTAL	60%	40%

POSSIBLE SOURCES OF CONFLICT

Discrimination remains a concern for the future of Indians in this country. Discrimination and "glass ceilings" in the workplace, for instance, have recently become an issue as professionals find themselves unable to rise beyond middle management positions, despite numerous years of employment with the same company. Another facet of discrimination is the incidence of hate-crime or other acts of violent racism. According to activist Ankur Goel, "While other Asian groups may have approached and crossed the point of local intolerance long ago, Indians are just now getting there".[1] The most well-known example of such intolerance occurred in Jersey City in 1987, when a group of youths known as the "dotbusters" (in reference to the cosmetic dot or *bindi* worn by Indian women on their foreheads) attacked and killed an Indian man.

Several interviewees of both the first and second generation referred to negative backlash against Indians in Fiji and Uganda and current mistreatment of Indians in Great Britain as scenarios they feared in the United States. Awareness and activism seem to be the means by which to combat the escalation of such persecution. Other future sources of conflict may stem from within the community, especially if two primary concerns are not addressed: differences between groups based on regional

[1] *Goel, 11/1/89*

background and the sense of alienation between the first and second generations.

COMMUNITY OF THE FUTURE

A plausible structure of the Indian community of the future will be one in which the first generation, the second generation, an increasing number of blue-collar Indians, and a newer wave of professionally educated immigrants from India will form different layers. Several interviewees guessed that it would be the new professional immigrants who will assume the leadership role previously held by the post-1965 professional immigrants. It is quite feasible that the new generation of professional immigrants will direct the community in much the same way as the earlier immigrants, continuing to maintain a strong tie to India. Many believe that the second generation's distinct concerns will lead them to initiate organizations separate from those of the newer immigrants.

CREATING IDENTITIES TO CELEBRATING IDENTITIES

Numerous ways have been discussed to help both generations of Indian-Americans through their current and continuing crossroads. The process of reconciling all that is Indian and all that is American and all that is neither in the lives of both immigrants and their children will be ongoing, as both groups continue their struggle with self-identification.

This work was originally titled "Celebrating Identities," emphasizing the ideal of coming to terms with Indian-American identity and visibly celebrating it. This celebration remains an ideal as Indian immigrants and their children continue to create and appreciate each other's identities. For these families, reconciling identity will not result in a finished product or the end of a struggle. Rather, identification signifies an ongoing *process.*

Comments from individuals in both samples illustrate a commitment to this process: Said Nirod, 52, father of three, "I really want my kids to have the best of both cultures. I know that they cannot think exactly like my wife and I because they are a product of their own environments. I think they should be allowed to develop in their own way, and I am proud of them for doing it."

Said Neel, 21, "I love and respect my parents more and more. Their intelligence and hard work reveal America to me in new ways, and their courage gives me hope to face my own future. I understand their identity, and, now, after many years of not liking who I was, I am starting to figure out who I am and am starting to like myself."

Awareness of the need to move toward creating an identity, a modified and more practical Indian-American identity, is a concrete and meaningful step. The ultimate goal for both first and second generation Indians may indeed be to combine creation with celebration.

Appendix A: The Samples

Interviews were conducted with two distinct samples—first and second generation. I designed separate questionnaires for each group (See Appendix B). There were 120 individuals in each sample, each consisting of 60 males and 60 females.

Much of the sample was taken from Southern California, specifically the greater Los Angeles area. According to the first reports of the 1990 Census, there are 159,973 Indian individuals residing in California, representing a 176.3% increase in population since 1980. The study is balanced to reflect the situations of Indians throughout the nation, as it includes interviews with community leaders from all over the United States as well as data from national conferences, forums, and publications.

The objective of this aspect of the study was to isolate a sample of people who reflected the characteristics of the post-1965 professional Indian population in the United States. Thus, those selected for the sample had to have the following characteristics: concentration in managerial and professional occupations, high levels of education, and, consequently, high median household incomes.

Southern California seemed to be the logical choice from which to take much of the sample as it is similar to other areas in the United States with substantial professional Indian populations (namely, New York and Illinois) in terms of choice of residence for immigrants, income-level, and education-level. The January 1988 *Asian and Pacific Islander Special Report*, for instance, indicates the following:

- In the greater L.A. area, the highest percentages of Indians were employed in managerial and professional occupations (43%) and technical, sales, and administrative support occupations (36.6%).

- In the greater L.A. area: of 7330 Indian males, 87.1% were high school graduates, and the median years of schooling was 16.3. Of 6958 females, 71.0% were high school graduates, and the median years of schooling was 12.9.

- The median income of an Indian household in the greater L.A. area was $20,127, and the mean was $24,449.

The sample could be criticized on the basis that it consisted predominantly of Southern California Indians. Some may argue that generally higher levels of affluence, the cosmopolitan nature of the population, as well as a more relaxed, "laid-back" attitude may have made responses of Southern California Indians different from those of other Indians in the United States. Given their characteristics, nevertheless, one may conclude that Indian professional families in Southern California are generally typical of Indian professional families in other parts of the country.

The first generation sample was randomly chosen based on the following criteria: both husband and wife had to have at least a bachelor's degree, and one individual (husband or wife) had to have a degree in a professional field. Furthermore, they had to have immigrated to the United States between 1965 and 1980 and had to have at least one child. Names of individuals were obtained from directories of Indians living in various parts of Southern California and also through "word-of-mouth." The following tables present some of the first generation sample raw data:

TABLE A.1

AGE OF FIRST GENERATION SAMPLE

	30-40	41-45	45-50	50 or over
Male	8%	25%	37%	30%
Female	25%	48%	17%	10%

TABLE A.2

FIELD IN WHICH RECEIVED FIRST PROFESSIONAL DEGREE

	Medicine	Engineering and Related	Business	No Professional Degree
Male	30%	57%	13%	0%
Female	15%	27%	10%	48%

TABLE A.3

PERCENTAGE WHO RECEIVED HIGHER FORMAL EDUCATION IN THE U.S.

Male	87%
Female	28%

TABLE A.4

REASON HUSBAND & WIFE ORIGINALLY IMMIGRATED (Sample of 60)

Higher Education	Economic Opportunity	Family In U.S.	Political
53%	30%	12%	5%

The second generation sample also was randomly chosen. It consisted of individuals from 18 to 25 years old, and names were selected from directories of university "India Clubs" and through "word-of-mouth." The main criteria for this group was that at least one parent had to hold a professional degree and had to have immigrated in the wake of the 1965 Immigration Act.

TABLE A.5

AGE OF SECOND GENERATION SAMPLE

	18-20	21-23	24-25
Male	18%	65%	17%
Female	30%	55%	15%

Appendix B: The Questionnaires

The following questionnaires were designed for each sample. All interviews were done in person, but not every question was asked of every individual interviewed.

First Generation Questionnaire

I. BACKGROUND

A. Personal
1. Sex, age, education, family (spouse, children, etc.)
2. Background in India (region, religion, language used at home).
3. Professional (employment) background

B. Associations
1. What does your regional and/or religious affiliation mean to you? Does it affect your choice of whom you associate with?
2. How do you feel about people belonging to other regions or religions?
3. To what racial or ethnic group do most of your friends belong? (IF INDIAN) From what region in India do most of them hail? What religion?

C. Immigrant Background/Self-definition
1. Why and when did you come to the United States?
2. At what point did you consider "immigrating" and why?
3. What were your images of the U.S. before you arrived? Has your experience, thus far, met those images?
4. Characterize the typical Indian immigrant to the U.S. of the "1965 crop." Why do you think they immigrated? Are you typical or different from this characterization?
5. What, if anything, makes them different from other early immigrants to the U.S.? What, if anything, makes them different from other recent (1965 and after) immigrants to the U.S.?
6. Since you came to the U.S., how often have you returned to India? How long have you stayed? Who goes with you? Do you plan to continue these visits?

7. Do you think of yourself as being in a particular social class? Which one?

8. Are there different classes within the Indian community in the U.S.? Which one do you consider yourself to be in?

9. At this point, do you plan to return to India permanently? (IF YES) At what age? Did you when you first immigrated?

II. POLITICS

A. Political Involvement While Living in India

1. What was the level of your family's political involvement in India? Did you participate directly, indirectly, or neither?

2. Were national and international political issues routinely discussed in your household while you were growing up in India?

3. What was your family's political affiliation in India?

4. How does one become "politically involved" in India?

5. How regularly did you or your family vote during Indian elections?

6. What did it mean to you that India was a democracy?

B. Political Involvement in U.S.

1. Would you say you are more interested in international affairs, national affairs, or local affairs? Why? •

2. Do you routinely discuss political issues at work? At home? Indian or American? National or international?

3. What is your understanding of democracy in the United States? Does it differ from democracy in India?

4. How does one become "politically involved" in the U.S.?

5. When you think of American politicians, what do you think of? Why would someone go into politics? *

6. Are there any politicians or people in American government that you admire? Who? Why? Are there any that you dislike? Who? Why? *

7. Do you think political leaders care about the way people like you feel? *

8. Do you ever feel that U.S. politics and government are so complicated that you don't understand what's going on? How often do you feel that way?

9. Do you wish you were more politically aware or are you satisfied with your level of awareness?

10. What kinds of issues are important to you and why?

11. How would a person like you take action on these issues if they chose to?

C. Attitudes Toward Indian Politics

1. Do you keep up with Indian politics? How? Why?

2. Does India's international status have any relevance to your status as an Indian living abroad?

3. What is your opinion of American foreign policy with respect to India? Of Indian foreign policy with respect to America? Do you feel that India-U.S. relations are important to you and your future? Why or why not?

III. CIVIC AND SOCIAL PARTICIPATION AND ATTITUDES

1. Are you involved in any organizations of Indians residing in the United States? (IF YES) Which ones? For how long have you been involved? In what capacity? (IF NO) Why?

2. Are you involved in any non-Indian organizations? (SAME FOLLOW UP QUESTIONS AS ABOVE)

3. Do you participate or volunteer for any activity or organization in any capacity (INCLUDES CHILDREN'S SPORTS, SCHOOL, ETC.)?

IV. DISCRIMINATION

A. General

1. Have you ever been discriminated against? (IF YES) In what way? By whom?

B. General Sense of Equality and Justice

1. Are there people that you see as "better" than you? Who? How? Are there people you feel better than somehow? How? Who? *

2. Would you say that you are generally treated justly by the national government? Are you treated fairly at work? In society in general? By your coworkers and neighbors? *

3. Do you feel that there are any kinds of people who get special treatment according to the law? Are there people who are discriminated against by the law? *

C. Stereotyping

1. How would you stereotype an Indian immigrant? Do you feel others perceive Indians in this way?

2. What is your understanding of the "Asian stereotype"? Do you feel this stereotype *can* be applied to Indians? Do you feel that it *is* being applied to Indians?

3. Are Indians, in your opinion, "Asians"? Do you feel that others categorize Indians as "Asians"?

D. Work Life

1. Describe your job

2. Background: How and where did you start your career? How many times have you switched jobs? What were the different stages that got you to where you are now?

3. What factors contributed to your success? Are these the same factors that have contributed to the success of other Indians?

4. What factors do you think contribute to the professional success of the non-Indian people you are acquainted with?

5. If you were the boss, what criteria would you use to promote people? *

6. Are you satisfied with the level you are currently at professionally?

7. Are there any barriers keeping you from attaining your professional goals?

V. SECOND GENERATION

A. Identity and Loyalty

1. Many non-white children are asked the question by their peers and others, "what are you?" - presumably meaning, what is your ethnic or racial background. How would you answer this question for your children? How do you think they would answer?

2. Do you feel that it is more important for the second generation of Indians in America to identify with their Indian background or to attempt to "blend in" with American society?

3. Are most of your children's friends, to your knowledge, Indian or non-Indian? Do they, in your opinion, feel more comfortable with Indian or non-Indian peers?

4. If your children have ever visited India before, how did they react? How did others react to them?

5. Are your children "happier" or better off than you were during your childhood in India? Do they have a more or less promising future than you did?

6. What do you think of the "ABCD" (American Born Confused *Desi*) label? Is it accurate? What do your children think of it?

7. What are your concerns, if any, regarding your children? What are you most satisfied about regarding your children?

B. Social Issues
1. What are your views regarding the second generation and dating?

2. Many people prefer that their children marry someone from the same ethnic group. How do you feel about that?

3. Do you think that most of the second generation will eventually marry other Indians or non-Indians?

4. Do you and your children discuss issues such as dating and marriage?

5. What are your views on returning to India to find a spouse?

C. Ambitions for Children
1. Is there any specific occupation your children want to pursue when they are adults? What would you like them to do? Why? *

2. Do you think they'll succeed? (IF YES) Why? (IF NO) What do you think they will do when they are adults? *

3. How well-off do you think your children will be compared to you? How do you feel about that? *

4. Describe the ideal situation you would like to see your children in when they are adults. Will they attain this? How?

5. How will non-Indians perceive Indians when your children get ready to enter the workforce?

D. Children Socializing Parents
1. How much, if any, and in what instances do the opinions and needs of your children influence your opinions and actions?

VI. ETHNICITY/ASSIMILATION
1. What is your conception of the "melting pot?" Did this apply when you first arrived or immigrated? Does it apply today?

2. What does it mean to assimilate into American society? Can Indians do this? Do you want to do this?

3. Under what circumstances do you or will you feel most integrated into American society? Least integrated?

4. Can Indians be involved in American society without forsaking their culture and ethnic identity? How?

5. Of all the aspects of your culture, which do you want to retain the most? Which do you feel least strongly about retaining?

VII. ATTITUDES

1. Would you say that you are happier or less happy now than you were when you first immigrated to the U.S.?

2. If you had the choice of whether or not to immigrate to make again, what would you choose?

3. If you imagined your future in the worst possible light, what would it look like? Do you think this is likely to happen? Can you prevent this from happening? *

4. How do see the future of Indians in this country?

*   Taken from Robert Lane's *Political Ideology*
*   Taken from Jennifer Hochschild's *What's Fair?*

SECOND GENERATION QUESTIONNAIRE

I. BACKGROUND
1. Sex, age, education, family (members, profession, etc.)
2. Where born
3. Region/religion parents from in India
4. When and under what circumstances did your parents immigrate from India? What do you know or what are your impressions of their immigrant experience?

II. TIES TO INDIA
1. Do you speak or understand your native language? (IF YES) With whom do you speak the language? (IF NO) Do you wish you did?
2. Have you ever visited India? (IF YES) How many times? What were your reactions? What were others' reactions to you?
3. Do you or your parents ever plan to settle in India permanently? (IF YES) When? Why?
4. Do the difficulties that India faces concern you?
5. How do you feel about India, in general?

III. IDENTITY AND LOYALTY
1. Have you ever been asked the question "what are you?" - presumably meaning what is your racial or ethnic background? (IF YES) How did you answer? What would your parents say if they were answering for you?
2. Do you feel that it is more important for you to identify with your Indian background or to attempt to "blend in" with American society? What are you doing?
3. To what racial or ethnic group do most of your friends belong?
4. Do you feel more comfortable with Indian or non-Indian peers? Do your parents prefer that you associate with one group over the other?
5. Would you say that there are certain things about you that your non-Indian friends fail to understand because they have a different cultural background?
6. If you have Indian friends, to what region or religion do most of them belong?

7. What do you think of the "ABCD" (American Born Confused *Desi*) label? Is it accurate? What do your parents think of it?

IV. SOCIAL ISSUES

1. What are views toward dating and marriage? How do your views differ from those of your parents?
2. Do you discuss issues such as dating and marriage with your parents? Do you feel your parents are receptive to your views?
3. What type of marriage would you prefer?
4. What are your views toward returning to India to find a spouse?

V. AMBITIONS

1. What would you like to pursue - education, career, etc.?
2. Is there any specific career your parents would like you to pursue? Why?
3. Would you consider a career other than the one your parents suggest to you?
4. Do you think you will succeed in your career choice? Why?
5. On what criteria do you think you will be judged in terms of admissions to schools and colleges and job opportunities?
6. How well-off do you think you will be compared to your parents? How do you feel about that?
7. Will you have a harder or easier time succeeding than your parents? Why?
8. Is it your parents' responsibility to see that you are educated and settled in life? What can they or have they done to help you?
9. Are you or have you been "happier" or better off than your parents were during their childhoods in India? Do you have a more or less promising future than they did?
10. Describe the ideal situation you would like to see yourself in when you are an adult. Will you attain this? How?
11. How will non-Indians perceive Indians when you get ready to enter the workforce?
12. What, if any, are the concerns of your generation of Indians in America? What are you most satisfied about?

VI. SOCIALIZING PARENTS

1. How much, if any, and in what instances do your opinions and needs affect your parents' opinions and actions?

2. On what issues do you agree with your parents? On what issues do you disagree?

VII. POLITICAL, CIVIC, SOCIAL INVOLVEMENT

A. American Politics

1. Do you routinely discuss political issues at school/work? At home? Indian or American? National or international?

2. What is your understanding of democracy in the United States?

3. How does one become politically involved in the U.S.?

4. Do you think political involvement is important? Do your parents agree or disagree with you?

5. Do you see yourself as getting politically involved as an adult? Would you consider a career in politics or public service? (IF YES) Would you get involved as a member of the Indian community or as a member of mainstream U.S.?

6. What, if any, is your political affiliation? Does yours differ from your parents'?

7. What kinds of issues are important to you and why? What issues are important to your parents and why?

8. How would a person like you take action on these issues if you wanted to?

9. Are there any politicians or people in American government that you admire? Who? Why? Are there any that you dislike? Who? Why?

10. Do you think political leaders care about the way people like you feel?

B. Attitudes Toward Indian Politics

1. Do you keep up with Indian politics? Do your parents? How? Why?

2. Does India's international status have any relevance to your status as a person of Indian origin?

3. What is your opinion of American foreign policy with respect to India? Of Indian foreign policy with respect to America? Do you feel that India-U.S. relations are important to you and your future? Why or why not?

C. Attitudes Toward Civic and Social Participation

1. Are you involved in any organizations or clubs in or outside of school? (IF YES) Which ones? For how long have you been involved? In what capacity?

2. Are you involved in any non-Indian organizations? (SAME FOLLOW UP QUESTIONS AS ABOVE)

3. Do the social problems of India concern you? (IF YES) Which problems? What could you do about them?

VIII. DISCRIMINATION

A. General

1. Have you ever been discriminated against? (IF YES) In what way? By whom?

2. Are Indians in the U.S., in general, discriminated against to a greater or lesser degree compared to other groups? Specify.

B. Stereotyping

1. How would you stereotype an Indian immigrant? Do you feel others perceive Indians in this way? How would you stereotype a second-generation Indian? Do others perceive them in this way?

2. What is your understanding of the "Asian stereotype?" Do you feel this stereotype *can* be applied to Indians? Do you feel that it *is* being applied to Indians?

3. Are Indians, in your opinion, "Asians?" Do you feel that others categorize Indians as "Asians?"

IX. ETHNICITY/ASSIMILATION

1. What is your conception of the "melting pot?" Did it, in your opinion, apply when your parents immigrated? Does it apply today?

2. What does it mean to assimilate into American society? Can Indians do this? Do you want to do this?

3. Under what circumstances do you or will you feel most integrated into American society? Least integrated?

4. What is more important for you: assimilating into American society or maintaining your culture? For your parents?

5. Can Indians be involved in American society without forsaking their culture and ethnic identity? How?

X. ATTITUDES

1. If your parents had the choice of whether or not to immigrate to make again, and you could influence that choice, which would you like them to choose?

2. If you imagined your future in the worst possible light, what would it look like? What about your parents' future? Do you think this is likely to happen? Can you prevent this from happening?

3. How do you see the future of Indians in this country?

BIBLIOGRAPHY

Agarwal, Priya. "Peninsula Chinese Community May Total 10,000." *Palos Verdes Peninsula News* (7/15/89), p. 1.

Agarwal, Priya. "Hard Work is Key to Korean Success." *Palos Verdes Peninsula News* (7/20/89), p. 1.

Agarwal, Rajiv. "Raising Indian Children in U.S." *India Abroad* (3/15/91), p. 3.

Allis, Sam. *Time*, Vol. 137, No. 12 (3/25/91), pp. 64-66.

Assisi, Francis. "The Indo-American Lives a Marginal Existence," in *Indo- Americans: A Historical Perspective and Glimpses of Exhibition* (San Jose: 6th Biennial National Convention of National Federation of Indian American Associations, 1990).

Basu, Rekha. "American Born Confused 'Desis.'" *India Today*, Vol. XIV (8/31/89), pp. 98-100.

Bureau of the Census. *Asian and Pacific Islander Special Report.* Volume 2, January 1988.

Chandrasekhar, S. (ed.). *From India to America.* La Jolla: Population Review Publications, 1986.

DeVos, George. "Ethnic Pluralism: Conflict and Accommodation," in George De Vos and Lola Romanucci-Ross (eds.), *Ethnic Identities and Cultural Continuities and Change* (Palo Alto: Mayfield Publishing Co., 1975.

Goel, Ankur J. "Are Indian-American Men Sexist?" *India West* (10/12/90), p. 54.

Goel, Ankur J. "Asian Indians: Crossing the Point of Intolerance." Personal Statement, National Congressional Conference on Anti-Asian Violence, 11/1/89.

Goel, Vindu. "Two Identities, One Person." *Awaaz*, Spring 1988.

Helweg, Arthur W. and Helweg, Usha M. *An Immigrant Success Story: East Indians in America.* Philadelphia: University of Pennsylvania Press, 1990.

Hochschild, Jennifer L. *What's Fair?* Cambridge: Harvard University Press, 1986.

IRCD Bulletin. Vol. XV, Numbers 1-2, Winter/Spring 1988, p. 8.

Juthani, Nalini. "Conflicts and Compromises as Experienced by Indians," in Jyoti Barot and Jagat Motwani (eds.), *Conference on Youth and Family* (San Jose: Sixth Biennial National Convention of Indian-Americans, 1990).

Lacher, Irene. "No Fear He May Offend." *L.A. Times* (5/25/90), p. E1.

Making Waves: An Anthology of Writings By and About Asian American Women. Boston: Beacon Press, 1989.

Mukherjee, Bharati. *Darkness.* New Delhi: Penguin Books, 1990.

Murarka, Ramesh. "Rap for Youth Awards Night." *India West* (7/6/90), p. 44.

Njeri, Itabari. "Beyond the Melting Pot." *L.A. Times.* (1/13/91), p. E1.

Perkash, Arunadhati. "Raising Children in Two Cultures," in *6th Biennial National Convention of National Federation of Indian American Associations* (San Jose, 1990).

Radia, Chandu. "Closer Look at Indian Culture." *India Abroad* (4/5/91), p.3.

Rajgopal, J. "The X + 1 Syndrome." *The Economic Times,* Bombay (1/6/88).

Saran, Parmatma. *The Asian Indian Experience in the United States.* Cambridge: Schenkman Books, Inc., 1985.

Sikri, Aprajita. "The Fortune 2nd Generation." *India Abroad* (10/13/89), pp. 16-19.

Sowell, Thomas. *Ethnic America.* New York: Basic Books, Inc., 1981.

Sterba, James P. "Indians in U.S. Prosper in Their New Country, And Not Just in Motels." *Wall Street Journal* (1/27/89), p. 1.

Takaki, Ronald. St*rangers From a Different Shore.* Little, Brown and Company, 1989.

Wolfinger, Raymond E. *The Politics of Progress.* New Jersey: Prentice Hall, Inc., 1974.